Ms.—ARCHITECT

WESTMINSTER PRESS BOOKS
BY
D. X. FENTEN

Ms.—Architect

Ms.—Attorney

Ms.—M.D.

The Making of a Police Officer

Ms.–ARCHITECT

By
D. X. FENTEN

THE WESTMINSTER PRESS
Philadelphia

Book Design by Dorothy Alden Smith

First Edition

Published by The Westminster Press®
Philadelphia, Pennsylvania

PRINTED IN THE UNITED STATES OF AMERICA

9 8 7 6 5 4 3 2 1

Library of Congress Cataloging in Publication Data

Fenten, D   X
    Ms.—architect.

    Includes index.
    SUMMARY: Examines the traditionally subordinate
place of women in architecture and discusses career
opportunities for women as architects and in related
jobs.
    1. Women architects—United States—Juvenile
literature. 2. Architecture—Vocational guidance—
Juvenile literature. [1. Women architects.
2. Architecture—Vocational guidance. 3. Vocational
guidance] I. Title.
NA1997.F4   720'.23   77–7498
ISBN 0–664–32615–3

CONTENTS

PREFACE

You're a young woman and you are interested in architecture. All the things you know and have heard about it make it seem like the perfect career for you. But you've heard other things —lots of talk that makes you wonder.

"Women architects are O.K. They're fine for pretty kitchens, but big buildings, really big projects, should be left for the men."

"Women are too petty. They just can't grasp the bigger picture. They're fine for other professions, but not for architecture."

That has been the attitude among males in the profession for the past twenty to twenty-five years. This overwhelmingly male profession was not, to say the least, making women feel wanted, welcome, or even competent.

However, in architecture, as in other professions, times, attitudes, and percentages are changing. Up-to-date comments sound more like:

"The word has gotten out that women in architecture are having their day. One of the prejudices—that women did not have the physical stamina or coordination necessary to make it—has waned considerably. Women have shown themselves to have everything needed to succeed in this profession . . . and are no longer afraid to 'show up' the male students to prove it."

"Everyone has thought and said that a woman must be extraordinary to succeed in the professions. Only a superwoman could make it to the top, especially in architecture, was the feeling. That's hogwash. Now, anyone who wants it and is willing to work for it can make it."

These comments, from leading professors of architecture, are what this book is all about. If men have "the stuff" of which architects are made, then women have it too. There are many fine male architects, but there are also some mediocre ones. Women have the right and now have the opportunities to think about, get the education for, and succeed in this profession.

This will not be a cheerleading pep talk designed as a recruitment piece for women in architecture. It will be, like our two other career books for women in this series (Ms.—M.D. and Ms.—Attorney), a careful examination of the facts, from all sides, buttressed by concrete suggestions from pros in the field. We hope many more women will investigate architecture as a career field, because we sincerely believe that women have much to contribute to the humanity of living and working environments, perhaps even adding a new and valuable dimension to the problem-solving that is architecture.

It is important to note that many well-known and respected female architects are growing tired of, and disgusted with, the sluggishness of their women colleagues in striving for the top, and of the almost total domination of the profession by men who are willing to climb higher on the executive ladder. They are also tired of being asked questions about what it's like being a woman architect, about the discrimination they may have encountered, about whether they would recommend their profession to their daughters or other women.

We thank these architects for awakening us to the idea that "it's enough already." They have had more than enough talk and questions. All they want is to get to the business of working as architects—not male architects or female architects, but as architects. They are all professionals, in an exciting, creative profession.

We would also like to thank all the people—architects, educators, engineers, builders, and many, many more—who were able to listen to our questions and supply the answers that ultimately made up this book. Special thanks go to all the societies, associations, and organizations that aimed us in the right direction and consistently supplied expertise, support, time, and large doses of encouragement.

Few of the quoted passages in this book are listed with full references. Naming them would serve little purpose, for though the speakers are recognized leaders in architecture, their names would not be familiar to the general reader. It is enough to know that they are all leaders and outstanding professionals who care deeply about their profession and took the time to try to help make it even better than it is.

It is customary for an author to thank the home team, and without them none of my books or other adventures would have been possible. It is also customary for writers and journalists to use the modest "we" when speaking of themselves. For me, it has never been a question of modesty, because my "we" is my wife, Barbara, and our children, Donna and Jeff, all of whom supply encouragement, enthusiasm, and love.

On the occasion of this our twenty-fifth book, some specifics are fun to mention. When we wrote the first "Ms." book *(Ms. —M.D.)*, Donna was a young girl who dreamed and spoke of one day being a doctor. Now she is a young woman entering college in a pre-med program. We thank her for her help, her comments, her smiling and sunny disposition which has grown as she has. We also appreciate her new professional skills— which include the typing of our final manuscripts.

As our writing has grown, so has our son, Jeff. We thank him for his contributions, which have always included the reading of all manuscripts intended for children of whatever age he happened to be at the time, with comments on what he liked and didn't like. In addition, his culinary skills have soared over the years (perhaps out of self-defense), and now, when deadlines are tight, we don't all starve. Jeff has become quite "the man in the kitchen."

Special thanks, once again, to Barbara, who is coauthor in fact if not in by-line.

9

Thanks, too, to the many readers who continue to believe that D.X. Fenten is a woman, writing for women. I can't think of a finer compliment. And, of course, to my friends at Westminster who smile broadly when speaking of their "feminist author."

D.X.F.

Greenlawn, New York

1

WHAT KIND OF NUMBER IS 3.7%?

Look at the statistics that follow and take your pick. They are all so ridiculous it doesn't matter which ones you choose. The U.S. Department of Labor reported that 3.8% of all architects in 1950 were women, 2.1% in 1960, and 3.6% in 1970. The 1970 Census showed that 3.7% of 57,081 architects were women.

Time magazine, in a special issue devoted to "The American Woman" in 1972, said, "Women architects have fared even worse than painters. Only 6% of the students in architecture schools are women and only 1% of the members of the American Institute of Architects (AIA)." Two years later, in 1974, *The New York Times* headlined a story, "Women Architects Building Influence in a Profession That Is 98.8% Male."

In 1976, after a careful and exhaustive study of women in architecture, the AIA reported:

"To begin with, there just aren't many women in the profession. According to the survey, only 1.2 percent of all registered architects are women, and only 3.7 percent of the entire architectural work force. This reflects traditional and persistent views of women in all careers and professions; but while the numbers of women with jobs, and the numbers of women entering professions, have been rising, the architectural profession still lags behind many other fields in opening opportunities for women.

"The number of women entering architectural schools is

increasing, but by small and uneven increments. A large part of the problem is that architecture has traditionally been presented to the public as a man's world.

"Those women who have become architects have reported a variety of discriminatory practices directed against them. Their salaries are lower than men's salaries—on the average, 28.64 percent lower. Advancement is another problem: for women it usually stops in the lower and middle echelons, although sometimes the work is the same as that being done by men with higher salaries and grander titles.

"Other discriminatory practices include discrimination against married women, women with young children, or women who become pregnant. In addition to these specific problems, there is the stumbling block of general sex discrimination manifesting itself in sexist language and in stereotypical ideas about women."

Why are there so few women in architecture? Why have they stayed away in droves when they have so much to offer? Ellen Perry Berkeley, an architect writing for *Architectural Forum,* says that the attitudes openly expressed in the schools offer a partial explanation:

"The dean of one Ivy League school of art and architecture was approached by a young woman at a party. 'I'm one of your students,' she said. He was trying to place her. 'In graphics?' he asked. 'No, architecture.' His reply was quick: 'Women shouldn't *be* in architecture.'

"The dean of another Ivy League school last year questioned his Committee on the Status of Women as to whether women should even be encouraged to enter the design professions 'because of the stamina involved.'

"A design critic at still another major school announced over TV that he couldn't take seriously a certain gifted woman in his class, since she would 'just go out and get married.'

"When the NYC Commission on Human Rights asked several Eastern architectural schools to recruit more women students, one dean was unenthusiastic, said *The New York Times.* 'Women approach architecture differently from men—they're either too finicky or too controlled,' he said.

"With these attitudes, a woman's application is likely to be very carefully scrutinized or very quickly dismissed. (One young woman tells of two schools 'losing' her application.)

But the problem begins earlier. Beatrice Dinerman's research discloses that "close to two thirds" of a representative group of women architects received no encouragement from counselors or faculty members to enter the profession; over half were "actively *discouraged*" from this choice.

Not a very pretty or encouraging picture. Did you ever hear the old joke, "Cheer up, things could be worse. So I cheered up and, sure enough, things got worse." Well, read on, because the picture of women in architecture gets worse. Moving along to women architects working in the field, Ms. Berkeley reports the following incidents that go beyond "acceptable" limits. Each is a true story, one of a growing number that women are gradually revealing about their professional lives:

"A British woman worked six years for a firm in the Boston area before attaining the level of responsibility she had enjoyed in Britain. She was not, however, made an associate. When she decided to move on, her projects were divided among several men, all associates in the firm.

"A woman who recently graduated from Yale and had almost a year's office experience was hired at a dollar an hour less than a man who had no experience. She asked him to speak to their employer but he declined, afraid he'd lose the dollar. At her insistence, the employer 'remedied' the situation, raising her hourly wage fifty cents. Another woman, registered for years, was doing the same work as men earning considerably more. When she asked for a raise she was told, 'What are you complaining about? You're the highest paid woman in the office.'

"In the Midwest, the gala dedication of a prominent public building was attended by John F. Kennedy, other dignitaries, and the male principals of the firm. The woman architect who designed the building was not invited.

"On a young designer's first visit to a project she had taken

JANE A. SHAPIRO, AIA

Women architects, given the opportunity, design and act as project architects for buildings that range from large industrial complexes to private homes, like these in Columbus, Ohio

over in mid-construction, the construction administrator from her office and the workmen took her up the outdoor service elevator at top speed, through open wells, and swinging over steel beams fourteen stories in the air. The woman learned later (not from the construction administrator) that this wasn't exactly standard practice.

"A new graduate from Cooper Union found herself increasingly asked to do secretarial work. When her employer decided to move the bulk of his practice to the suburbs and leave only one person in the city, he asked her to type this ad: 'Office to share with draftswoman who answers phones or whatever. . . .' She typed the ad, leaving out her own part of it and quit.''

Do these problems exist only when women start college or apply to architecture school? Do the problems continue to grow and reach their awful peak as women graduate and move into professional work situations? No, not by a long shot. The progression actually starts long, long before that. All you, the young woman reader, need to do is think back to the days when you were a little girl. The Federation of American Scientists (FAS) gives us all the proof we need to back up what we already knew:

''The process of selecting professionals in the field begins at an early age and girls are excluded. Aside from the well-documented difficulties with textbooks and curricula which beset elementary and high school education in general, girls who are interested in science are confronted with special problems. Almost every schoolchild has encountered the conventional wisdom that girls are interested in English and spelling, while boys are interested in math and sciences.

''This attitude surfaces in many ways. For example, a 1971 survey of 800 toys on supermarket shelves showed that boys are depicted sixteen times more often than girls on the packages of education toys. When a girl does make her way into the picture, the odds are fourteen to one against her participating in the use of the toy. Teachers reinforce such images of 'helpless females,' as the testimony of an eighth-grade New York City girl shows: 'Well, within my physics class last year, our teacher asked if there was anybody interested in being a lab assistant in the physics lab, and when I raised my hand he told all the girls to put their hands down because he was only interested in working with boys.'

''If a girl does not find support for her science interests from toys, teachers, principals, or special programs, where can she look? Unfortunately, it is often parents who make the situation even more crippling. The mystique of science puts them ill at ease. . . . An American Association of University Women survey of discrimination in May 1970 showed that 64 percent of

16

women and 41 percent of men believe that 'women are conditioned not to show their intelligence.' Parents certainly play an important role in this conditioning process, as do factors outside the home.''

So you have been brainwashed, conditioned, discriminated against, and aimed toward the "more feminine aspirations." Still want a career in architecture? If your answer is yes (and we're certain it is, or you wouldn't have read even this far), you'll need ammunition. You'll need lots of powerful ammunition to combat the myths and superstitions about working women that have developed and grown through the years. You may not have to fire a shot today or tomorrow, but it won't be long before you are faced with someone's inane remark or comment that makes you want to punch the person. Don't punch. Instead, let go with both barrels of information and statistics designed to send chauvinists of all kinds back to their foxholes.

A woman's place is in the home!

Homemaking, with the convenience of labor-saving devices, goods, and services, is no longer a full-time job. More than half of all women are in the labor force today and nine out of ten women *will* work outside the home.

It's not worth training a woman, because she'll only leave to get married or have children!

In fact, 23 percent of working women are single, and have a work life expectancy two years *longer* than the average male's. For women with children, the work life expectancy is twenty-five years.

Women work only for extra pocket money!

In 1972, about 42 percent of working women had no husband present. They were either single, widowed, divorced or separated, or had husbands who earned less than $3,000 per year. Another 21 percent had husbands with incomes between $3,000 and $7,000. They worked because of pressing economic need.

Women are ill more than male workers; they cost the company more!

A recent Public Health Service study shows little difference: 5.6 days a year for women, compared with 5.2 for men.

Most women whose children are still of school age remain at home with them!

Child care facilities exist and are being improved nationwide. Even lacking day care facilities, 12.7 million working women have children under eighteen. Of these, 4.4 million have children under six. We can see that about half of the mothers of school age children go to work as well as one third of those with preschool children.

Juvenile delinquency is caused by working mothers!

Studies show there are many causes of juvenile delinquency. Whether or not a mother works does *not* appear to be a determining factor.

Women should stick to "women's jobs" and should not compete for "men's jobs"!

Job requirements, with extremely rare exceptions, are unrelated to sex. Tradition, not job content, has made the distinction. In measuring twenty-two inherent aptitudes and knowledge areas, a research laboratory found that there is no sex difference in fourteen areas and, in the balance, women excel in six and men in only two.

18

Married women take jobs away from men!

In 1973 there were 19.8 million married working wives. The total number of unemployed men was 2.5 million. As you can see, if all the working wives quit, there would be a deficit in the labor force of 17.3 million workers, many of whom hold highly skilled and important positions for which men *could not* qualify.

Married women leave their jobs suddenly to move when their husbands do!

The U.S. Department of Labor's wage and labor standards administration states there are very small differences on job-leaving between men and women. Changing social patterns mean it is no longer necessary for a woman to leave *her* job because her husband is leaving *his* job. Also, "good" jobs for women are hard to come by, and if a woman has one, she is not in a hurry to leave it. Finally, flitting from job to job to follow her husband does not compile the type of job credentials a woman needs to get and keep a good job.

Women are not as well educated as men, so they should be paid less!

On the contrary, white women workers finished a median 12.5 years of schooling and white men 12.4; minority women 12.1 years and minority men 11.5.

Women don't want responsibility!

Relatively few women have been offered positions of responsibility. When they are, like the men, they cope with them in addition to personal or family responsibilities.

Men don't like to work for women supervisors!

Most men who complain about women supervisors have *never* worked for a woman. In one study, where at least three quarters of the male and female respondents (all executives) *had* worked with women managers, their evaluation of women was favorable. Interestingly, the study also showed that those who reacted unfavorably to women as managers showed a traditional cultural bias.

Still another survey showed that 41 percent of the reporting firms indicated that they hired women executives, and *none* rated their performance as unsatisfactory. Fifty percent of the respondents rated them as adequate, another 42 percent rated them the same as their predecessors. It's obvious that women have been doing something right, and should continue to think big.

But even with all sorts of right answers and all kinds of ammunition, you've got to be practical. You have your whole life in front of you. You must ask yourself the big question. Is there a future in architecture for women? Will you be able to get into a fine architecture school? Will college be a pleasant, rewarding experience, or will you wish you had chosen another field, one more "acceptable for women"?

And then, what about jobs once your formal schooling is over? Will there be jobs for women in architecture and will these jobs be worth having, worth striving for, worth bragging about? Is this the right time for women to get into architecture?

It certainly seems to be.

America's Bicentennial year saw another revolution—a revolution stirring and celebrating the awakening in the field of architecture to the inequities and injustices inflicted on women. This awakening, the result of tireless work by several outstanding women architects, was certainly a reason for celebration, but it was only a beginning. The course of action that is under way as a direct result of their labors is real cause for rejoicing.

First, in a policy statement on women in architecture the AIA said,

"The American Institute of Architects affirms that the architectural profession and the AIA are entirely and equally open to women and men.

"The AIA affirms that societal prejudices and the traditional views of the role of women are not justification for perpetuation of discriminatory treatment of women.

"The AIA shall make a determined effort to integrate women as full participants in the profession. To attain this goal the AIA shall take affirmative action during the next four-year period to:

"Increase the public's awareness of the contribution of women architects in the design of the built environment.

"Increase the percentage enrollment of women in all undergraduate and graduate architectural programs.

JANE A. SHAPIRO, AIA

The public needs to be aware that women contribute to the built environment with creative designs like this

"Promote employment policies and practices which will assure women equal access to employment opportunity.

"Increase the membership of women architects in the AIA.

"Insure active participation by women members in the activities of the AIA at all organizational levels.

"Any practices by AIA members that are found to deny women equal participation in the profession may be construed to be in violation of the Standards of Ethical Practice and policy of the American Institute of Architects and shall not be tolerated."

Then, in a statement sent to more than fifty thousand architects introducing the Affirmative Action Plan adopted by their organization, AIA President Louis de Moll said, in part:

"Implementation of this Affirmative Action Plan will require positive effort at every level—not only nationally but within chapters and state organizations, by firms, and by individual members—men and women.

"State components must take action to bring about changes in registration laws, and any other statutes governing practice and employment, which tend to discriminate against women in the profession.

"Chapters must make a particular effort to identify and recruit women professionals into their membership at every level. They must encourage the active participation by women members in chapter affairs, and particularly those areas of professional activity which are visible to the public through the news media—thus enhancing the visibility of women in architecture.

"Women members of the profession and the AIA must accept the task of creating greater awareness among various sectors of the public—including students and young people. By participating in career days, lecturing to college classes, and related activities, they can through their very presence encourage young women to consider careers in the design professions.

"Perhaps most important, principals in firms must wholeheartedly accept the responsibility for recruiting and hiring qualified women, for encouraging their professional development, and for providing the same financial incentives and advancement opportunities that are provided for male employees. . . .

"This is a commitment that all of us must consciously make —not merely as a matter of conscience, nor of compliance with governmental or other directives.

"If we fail to respond, we will be shortchanging not only a great many talented and dedicated architects and future architects. We will be shortchanging our whole profession."

Yes, this certainly seems to be the right time for you to get into architecture. This does not say that you will not face problems, but you will also face increased opportunities and advantages. A bit later on we'll see how the AIA and its architects are going about getting more women interested in and actually into architecture. For now, continue your interest in the field and see how the profession and women's roles in it have evolved throughout time.

2

STICKS AND STONES
TO STEEL AND GLASS

"Well, dear, you've done it again. I told you to move faster. Now all the good caves are gone. You'd better start thinking of something. We need some kind of protection from the weather, wild animals, and those wild animals you call your friends. We're the only family without a cave to call our own."

The caveman scratched his head, and using the most primitive stone tools, began to make a shelter. The human race had its first architect. As he lashed some branches together or piled stone on stone to make walls and a roof, we had the beginnings of what was to become known as architecture. From these meager beginnings, architecture had no place to go but up (no pun intended). And as these buildings started to go up, they reflected the needs, the beliefs, the environment, and the technical level of the civilizations doing the building.

For example, almost six thousand years ago, about the time of the Old Testament, the Egyptians, who believed in life after death, constructed the immense pyramids and other structures from the abundant stone of the Nile Valley. Designed to protect the dead as they moved into eternal life, these temples and tombs were built to last, and they did—so well, in fact, that we still marvel at them today.

At about the same time, the people of Mesopotamia believed in living for each day. They had little stone and timber, but plenty of the makings for bricks—clay, water, and sunshine. Their architecture was epitomized by the famous Hanging Gardens of Babylon, the terraced, pyramid-like temples, and the magnificent palace cities which, unfortunately, did not last long enough to be seen and enjoyed by our civilization. The Greeks with their perfect temples and the Romans with their forums and baths made distinctive contributions to the art and science of architecture. As the centuries rolled by, people from Europe and other parts of the world left their hallmarks on structures designed and built for a variety of reasons.

Where were the women throughout these formative ages of architecture? We can only guess they were behind the men who were the master designers and master builders—giving ideas and advice, suggestions and descriptions, on "how to make it better." Historical research reveals no famous early woman architect, builder, or designer. If women did any of this kind of work, it was a well-kept secret.

We can unwrap some of this secrecy if we jump down through time and land in our own country. In a "first of its kind" book called *From Tipi to Skyscraper: A History of Women in Architecture,* author-architect Doris Cole tells us, "The Indian women were the architects of their communities. Among many Indian tribes of North America, the women designed, fabricated, and constructed the dwelling units. In fact, architecture was often considered women's work."

It wasn't an isolated occurrence for a woman to do everything necessary to erect a shelter or a home. Women built the tipis, made the igloos, and constructed the pueblos. A closer look, for example, reveals that the women were not only the architects, they were just about everything else concerned with shelter. They designed the structures, gathered the materials, tanned the hides for covers, put the pieces together, erected them, and then took them down when camp was broken and the tribe moved on.

And they did a fantastic job. In describing the tipi, scholars have said that other tents were hard to pitch, hot in summer, cold in winter, badly lighted, unventilated, easily blown down, and—as if that wasn't enough—ugly also. But the conical tent, designed and erected by the women of the Plains Indian tribes,

25

has none of these faults. It can be pitched, if necessary, by a single person. It is roomy, well lighted, proof against high winds and heavy downpours, and, with its cheerful inside fire, snug in the severest winter weather.

Pioneer women were not nearly as involved in architecture as were the Indian women. Then toward the middle of the nineteenth century a new phenomenon arose—the domestic architecture book written by women. There were many written and many read, mostly by women. Though described as "etiquette" books, they were much more than that, being guides to assist early American women in making their homes and their lives a bit more comfortable and enjoyable.

A name that leaps out of the pages of these etiquette books is that of Harriet Beecher Stowe, who, with her sister Catherine Beecher, made all sorts of architectural suggestions to a legion of readers. Not only did the sisters supply information for beautifying a home, they got into the "nuts and bolts" of architecture, giving plans and descriptions for complete houses and for such systems as plumbing, heating, and ventilation. In *The American Woman's Home* (1869), Beecher and Stowe said, among other things:

"The main objection to attic rooms is their warmth in summer, owing to the heated roof. This is prevented by so enlarging the closets each side that their walls meet the ceiling under the garret floor.

"Aim to secure a house so planned that it will provide in the best manner for health, industry, and economy, those cardinal requisites of domestic enjoyment and success."

As an actual practitioner, Stowe had designed and had built her own house in Hartford, Connecticut. She felt almost as strongly about women in architecture as she did about slavery. About thirteen years after she wrote *Uncle Tom's Cabin,* she wrote *Household Papers and Stories.* In it she said, "One of the greatest reforms that could be . . . would be to have women architects. The mischief with houses built to rent is that they are all mere male contrivances. . . . Architecture and landscape gardening are arts every way suited to the genius of woman and

26

there are enough who have the requisite mechanical skill and mathematical education." She added, as a prod to men, "When women plan dwelling houses, the vast body of tenements to be let in our cities will wear a more domestic and comfortable air, and will be built more with reference to the real wants of their inmates."

Toward the end of the nineteenth century, women surfaced in architecture, though no one seemed to notice. In 1883 a monthly architecture magazine carried a story saying, "It is perhaps singular that in a time when nearly all the professions are invaded by courageous women . . . not one woman is found to try her fortune as an architect. There are women preachers and physicians and lawyers, as well as painters and sculptors, but no jealous architect finds a professional of the other sex."

Little did the speaker know that, at that very time, there were at least two women architects. In 1869, Harriet Morrison Irwin of North Carolina became the first woman to patent an architectural innovation for a dwelling. In 1881, Louise Blanchard Bethune of upstate New York became the first professional woman architect in the United States. These women as well as the ones that preceded them (unofficially) and the ones that followed (officially) proved that architecture, like medicine and law, needn't be a man's domain. They proved and continue to prove that if something must be designed and built for use by both women and men, it can surely be designed and built by either women or men.

Harriet Irwin, the sister-in-law of the South's "Stonewall" Jackson, watched the destruction wrought by the Civil War and, though she had no formal training, decided to make an architectural contribution to Reconstruction. Hiding a bit behind her initials, she patented in 1869, as "H. M. Irwin," an "Improvement in the Construction of Houses." She described her "revolution in the method of building houses":

"My invention consists of a dwelling-house or other building, hexagonal in form, and enclosing a space separated into hexagonal and lozenge-shaped rooms, . . . also of a chimneystack, arranged at the junction of the walls of the adjacent hexagonal rooms, and containing flues communicating with the fire-places in the several rooms.

"The objects of my invention are the economizing of space and building-materials, the obtaining of economical heating mediums, thorough lighting and ventilation, and facilities for inexpensive ornamentation."

Though her invention had validity, it did not create any mass movement toward hexagonal buildings divided by partitions into hexagonal and lozenge-shaped rooms. Undaunted, she continued the project to its logical conclusion by actually having the house built. It stood for over one hundred years in Charlotte, North Carolina, and may be standing still, as mute witness to the fact that if women are to live in houses, there is no reason why they should not design and build them.

About a dozen years later, probably totally unaware of the "revolution" of Mrs. Irwin, Louise Blanchard Bethune opened an architectural office in Buffalo, New York, and unfurled the banner of equality for women in the professions. She believed very strongly that women should be allowed to do whatever they were capable of doing, and should receive "equal pay for equal service." She was also convinced that if a woman was architecturally inclined, she should build whatever was needed, not only homes in which to live.

Bethune started out with the desire to attend the newly opened architecture course at Cornell University. But when an offer of a job as "draftswoman" with a Buffalo firm came up, she jumped at the chance. It was common knowledge that far more architects of her time were trained at the drafting table than in the lecture hall.

In five years she learned all she could, including that she wanted to spend the rest of her life married to an architect, Robert A. Bethune. In October, 1881, Bethune and Blanchard opened for business with a partnership boasting the first professional woman architect in the country. Two months later they changed the firm's name to R. A. and L. Bethune, a change in relationship causing a change in name.

The editors of *American Women of the Century* wrote in 1893:

"During the ten years of its existence the firm has erected fifteen public buildings and several hundred miscellaneous buildings, mostly in Buffalo and its immediate neighborhood. Mrs. Bethune has made a special study of schools and has been particularly successful in that direction, but refuses to confine herself exclusively to that branch, believing that women who are pioneers in any profession should be proficient in every department, and that now at least women architects must be

Florence Kenyon Hayden, one of the first U.S. women architects, and the building she designed in 1906. It is still in use—Oxley Hall on the Ohio State University campus

practical superintendents as well as designers and scientific constructors, and that woman's complete emancipation lies in 'equal pay for equal service.' Because the competition for the Woman's Building of the Columbia Exposition was not conducted on that principle, Mrs. Bethune refused to submit a design. The remuneration offered to the successful woman was less than half that given for similar service to the men who designed the other buildings. In 1885 Mrs. Bethune was elected a member of the Western Association of Architects . . . active in securing the passage of the Architects Licensing Bill, intended to enforce rigid preliminary examinations and designed to place the profession in a position similar to that occupied by medicine and law. In the last five or six years a dozen women have been graduated from the different architectural courses now open to them and Mrs. Bethune has ceased to be 'the only woman architect.' "

One of the young women graduated from "the different architectural courses now open to them" was the first woman graduate of the regular architecture course at the Massachusetts Institute of Technology, Sophia G. Hayden. After four years as a brilliant student at M.I.T., Hayden graduated as a Bachelor of Architecture in 1890.

Shortly thereafter, she read of "An Unusual Opportunity for Women Architects," and her decision to pursue the challenge was destined to change her life:

"Sketches are asked, on or before March 23, 1891, for the Woman's Building of the World's Columbian Exposition. None but those made by women will be considered. Applicants must be in the profession of architecture or have had special training in the same, and each must state her experience, in writing, to the Chief of Construction. . . . The selected design will carry with it the appointment of its author as architect of the building. She will make her working drawings in the Bureau of Construction, and receive an honorarium of $1,000 besides expenses. A prize of $500 and one of $250 will be given for the two next best drawings. A simple light-colored classic type of building will be favored. . . . The general outline of the building must follow closely the accompanying sketch plans, the extreme dimensions not exceeding two hundred by four hundred feet; exterior to be of some simple and definite style, classic lines preferred; the general effect of color to be in light tints. . . . First story, eighteen feet high; second story, twenty-five feet high . . . to come within the limit of . . . $200,000. The plans should show the outline desired, leaving all detail to the ingenuity of the competing architect, who is expected to give them a thorough study, locating openings, etc., so as to give easy access and exit to the constant flow of passing crowds. The main entrance will lead down a series of steps to the water landing.''

When the envelopes were opened, twenty-two-year-old Sophia Hayden was declared the winner. However, her moment of triumph was soon shattered by critics, plan modifications, and problem after problem. She met and conquered them all as designer, draftswoman, and construction supervisor, but at great personal cost. When the Woman's Building was formally opened in May, 1893, the architect was not present, for, it was reported, she had succumbed to ''brain fever'' or had collapsed from the ''responsibility for the execution of the prize-winning design.''

We The Women, which set out to show the achievements of outstanding American women in various fields, summarized the lives of Hayden and the other two early American women architects:

''The architect herself, despite her breakdown, was able in 1894 to prepare plans for a Memorial Building projected by the women's clubs of the country, and was able later on to marry an artist, William B. Bennett. Although she lived to the great age of more than eighty, however, she built no further buildings. . . . The building she had designed had stood, indeed, for an idea. Substantial, spacious, symmetrical, it had been, in its own special way, the 'bright particular star' in the crown of the Exposition that had pioneered a pathway for women. Harriet Irwin, who presented a book to the library of that building, Louise Bethune, who opposed the competition that led to its construction, and Sophia Hayden, who created it, all stood for an idea—the idea that architecture was yet another avenue along which women could walk, an avenue lined with lyrics if not epics in stone.''

The achievements of these women, working against almost unbelievable odds, did not cause any major shift in the feeling that architecture was man's work. Many new architecture schools resulted from the Land-Grant Act of 1862, which required these schools to be open to both men and women. But the feeling would persist into the twentieth century, bulwarked by administrators like the dean at a Big Ten school who answered a woman's request to study architecture in 1914 with the statement, "We don't want you, but since the school is coeducational and state-owned, we have to take you if you insist."

Even the beginning of the now famous, but all too short-lived, Cambridge School of Architecture and Landscape Architecture for women only dented, but never shattered, the feeling that "architecture is for men only, and if women must practice it, it should be only in the area of domestic architecture." This sort of discrimination has been carried down through the years despite formidable contributions by female architects. We will not detail these contributions here, except to include photographs of buildings done by both pioneering and contemporary women architects.

But despite the effectiveness of the design, the innovative techniques, the solutions to the problems presented, the superiority of the finished product, please note how few photographs there are, and realize that the lack is caused directly by the lack of female architects. Rectifying that situation will be your job. It is in your future, as *Ms.* magazine suggests, "to tackle the real question of architecture: how both sexes can liberate humankind from the stultifying cage of its built environment."

3
CAREER BUILDING BLOCKS

"To receive an education," says Catholic University, "is a misnomer if ever there was one. You are *offered* an education and you can *take* an education, but you can't *receive* an education."

Nowhere is this more true than in architecture, all the way from high school to graduate school. To receive is a passive act —and there is nothing passive about architecture. Sit and wait for information to come to you, sit and wait for opportunities to come to you, sit and wait for education to come to you, and you will have spent your life doing nothing but sitting and waiting. You will grow very old, very tired, and very disappointed. You will also have accomplished absolutely nothing.

Architecture demands that you have a detailed understanding of a great many subjects, some of which we rarely associate with architecture. It is a broad, dynamic, exciting, exacting field, and the more dynamic and exciting you are, the better you will fare.

Today an architect must be expert in science, technology, behavioral science, sociology, economics, ecology, politics, psychology, and business management—to name just a few. Scare you away because you feel you can't be expert in everything? Don't scare so easily, not if you really want a career in architecture.

The AIA is quick to point out that architects, like people in any other business or profession, have varying strengths and weaknesses. All have some artistic talent, but some more than others. Some are better managers—or better researchers. And so it is. There is, however, plenty of room in the profession for those with special interest and talents.

This national professional organization admits that even architectural educators have trouble defining the mixture of traits that make a good architect. Of course, they look for the bright student, whose overall academic record is good, but they look for other qualities too. Can you handle details without getting completely hung up in them? Can you work in a fairly unstructured situation without coming unglued? Do you really see the people and things you look at? Do you care? Are you analytical? Creative? Orderly? Original? Any of the above?

If you thought architecture was just designing big buildings, we had better talk a bit more about it so you will understand why you must be a "go-getter."

When we asked the AIA, "What do architects do?" and "What is the job really like?" We got several answers. The architects of the AIA explained that, in a typical situation, the architect would accept a commission from a client—a person, a board of directors, a government agency—to solve a problem. The problem might include the design of one single building, a group of buildings, many buildings and the spaces between them, or even a whole metropolitan area.

In addition, the practicing architect could be teaching future architects; developing new tools, materials, or systems to help other architects practice more efficiently or creatively; or working to create the kind of atmosphere where good design can happen on every level, from the city council to the U.S. Congress.

Architects are designers. They visualize, plan, relate, select, discard, synthesize. Architects draw. They provide plans, from simple, freehand "bubble diagrams" meant only to show relationships between spaces, to complete, detailed working drawings which the contractor and subcontractors will follow during construction.

In addition to these two often obvious things, we find that

34

architects must also be qualified to:

—**write.** Besides all the correspondence and other administrative paperwork that goes with any business, architects prepare written documentation of their projects; help clients organize their space needs and get them down on paper; write material for brochures and presentations; produce articles for professional magazines.

—**talk.** Architects make presentations to prospective and established clients; discuss and synthesize complex design problems and alternative solutions with other members of the design team; appear as expert witnesses before zoning boards,

M.I.T.

A rap session at Massachusetts Institute of Technology just before students will commit project ideas to paper. Analysis of details and thinking out loud are important to an architect's education

35

planning commissions, and legislative bodies—architects are constantly conferring, explaining, teaching, persuading. The ability to get ideas across clearly and forcefully is essential—if you're eloquent, that's a bonus.

—**figure.** Architects have to be able to calculate reliable budgets; they must be able to understand stresses on structures, to make sure their buildings will be safe. More and more offices are using computers to speed up some of the necessary calculations, but a computer can't help much unless you understand what you want it to do, and how.

—**manage.** Architects must manage their design projects— from the small scale of the design process to the larger scale of the completed development/design/construction process. During construction, the architect's office provides field representatives who visit the site frequently, check on progress, authorize payments, help the contractor interpret drawings— again, a kind of management. (In a small firm, the chief designer may turn into the on-site job superintendent merely by putting on a hard hat.) They must also manage the operations of their firms, which are usually partnerships or corporations.

Lots to learn, plenty to experience, no time to waste. Start right now. If you're in high school, start gathering information immediately. Decide in your own mind that you are interested in architecture and don't be dissuaded. If there is any dissuading to be done, you do it yourself, after all the facts are in and you've made up your own mind.

Beware of guidance counselors. The Federation of American Scientists reports, "High school counselors are, if anything, less informed, and less encouraging to young *girls* than teachers and parents."

A study prepared by the office of the Pennsylvania Secretary of Education revealed that

"Counselors tend to emphasize segregation of the sexes with the result that they pursue 'tracking practices which tend to place boys in advance sections of math and science and girls in sections of office practice.'

"Counselors look on the educational needs of girls 'with less urgency, based on the traditional image of a female's life: school, marriage, a family.'

" 'Many counselors hold rather strong views concerning the sexual origin and basis of certain aptitudes, based on normative data which indicated differences. . . . Consequently, occupational or educational fields requiring certain aptitudes become linked in the counselor's mind with the sexual differences she or he sees in the test results.' "

The Association of Collegiate Schools of Architecture (ACSA) advises potential architects that if counselors or teachers start giving a big lecture about what architecture school is going to be like, one should ask them where they are getting their information. They could be making it up. The only way to know for sure what architectural education is like today is to enroll and find out. Otherwise, all you are getting is hearsay.

Of course, before you do any enrolling, you must first complete your high school education and get your diploma. A few suggestions if you still have a few more terms to go in high school: The name of the game in preparing for an education in architecture is basics. Get as many basic liberal arts courses as you can before moving on to the design and technical courses that fill the college curriculum. Cram as many math, physics (chemistry is good, but physics is better), social studies, and communications (English) courses into your program as you can. If you have a choice of English courses, select the ones that specialize in composition rather than in grammar and literature.

Next on the list are the humanities courses. As we said, college will be full of design and technical courses, so take some history and language courses before you get there. It would seem that drafting courses would be a good idea in high school, but . . . The ACSA is rather outspoken about this, suggesting that you might take a high school drafting course just for fun. They caution that the person teaching it probably knows next to nothing about architecture. And if it's part of a "shop" course, you might as well forget it altogether.

The art courses probably won't do you much good unless

An award-winning architect doing some on-site job superintending in the rain and mud makes a suggestion about her design of the Belgian block fountain fed by roof-water runoff

they concentrate on freehand drawing. For an architect, next to talking, drawing is the most valuable motor skill, and you should try to get a head start on it. Drawing is like skiing or learning a language—the earlier you start, the better.

More positively, ACSA suggests that if you have a year or two of high school left, you should tell your teachers about your architectural ambitions and see if they can't tailor things a bit for you. For instance, your art teacher might help you by emphasizing freehand drawing instead of painting or ceramics. Also, your geography teacher might tell you something of the suitability of land for building—or better yet, some principles of urban geography. Your social studies teacher might offer you some special reading on how cities are shaped and by whom. Almost every subject has something of interest in it for future architects—if you ask for it.

And there are things you can do after school, during summer vacations or whenever you have some spare time. For example, the ACSA suggests:

Get a sketchbook and teach yourself to draw. Draw at least one thing a day, whether it's a plant, a person, or a building. You'll be discouraged at first, but after a while you'll be pleased with your new ability to express yourself. You can use a pencil or felt-tip or anything you want, but once you start using a particular medium, stick with it for a while. Not only will you learn to draw, it will also teach you *to see.* Remember, both perception and drawing are *learned* behavior. Although we are all born with hands and eyes, no one is born drawing or seeing. Also, learn how to use a camera if you have one—it's a very useful tool for an architect. But don't use it as a lazy way of drawing.

During summer vacations try to get a job either in an architecture-related company or in the construction business. Neither the kind of job nor the salary is important. All you want to do is learn a bit about the profession and see it close up. You can't help getting some valuable experience, learning some of the terminology and jargon, and sampling the profession you've chosen. You may become even more enchanted with the idea of becoming an architect, or you could find out that this profession is not for you. Whichever happens, this is the best time to find out.

While you're at it, and especially if jobs (at your level) are scarce in your area, check out the schools of architecture that run special summer orientation sessions. Enrolling in one of these would also give you a feel for what to expect in the "regular" architecture schools.

And, speaking of regular architecture schools, now is the time to pick one. It won't be an easy job (there are about one hundred of them in North America), but it is a job that must be done now.

Start by doing some homework. Surround yourself with the best books you can find on colleges and especially on architecture schools. Use the Appendix in this book as a starting point, and either send for the following books or borrow them from your school or local public library. All prices are as of 1976.

Architectural Schools in North America ($3)

Life Experiences in Environmental Design ($4)
Association of Collegiate Schools of Architecture
1735 New York Avenue, N.W.
Washington, D.C. 20006

Current List of Accredited Programs in Architecture (free)
National Architectural Accrediting Board, Inc.
(Same address)

NCARB Circulars of Information #1 and #4 (free)
National Council of Architectural Registration Boards
(Same address)

Careers in Architecture—Section 4, *Architects' Handbook of Professional Practice* ($1.30)
American Institute of Architects
(Same address)

Getting Into Architecture (free)
American Institute of Architects
(Same address)

Choose any or all of the latest editions of the following books to give you more detailed information about the specific colleges and universities in which you might be interested:

The College Handbook ($6.95)
College Entrance Examination Board
Educational Testing Service
Box 592, Princeton, N.J. 08540

Barron's Profiles of American Colleges ($6.95)
Barron's Educational Series, Inc.
113 Crossways Park Drive
Woodbury, N.Y. 11797

The alternative to using these reference materials is to survey all one hundred schools offering programs in one phase of architecture or another. That's no easy task, we can assure you, because that's exactly what we did to assemble the statistical information in the Appendix. For you, that is not necessary. Using the other sources, select a few schools by the process of elimination and then send for catalogs, bulletins, and admissions materials for these few. All of this should be done during the fall and winter of your junior year, so you'll have time to scout the schools and, if at all possible, to visit some during the spring months.

Be far more practical than romantic in your school selection process. Here are some of the questions you must ask yourself: Do you stand a chance of being accepted by a specific school —are your grades and test scores up to that school's standards? Can you afford the tuition, room and board, and miscellaneous other costs? Is there a chance of a scholarship or other financial assistance from the school? From your parents? Do the school's objectives in architecture fall close to those you had envisioned? Do they have the kind of program you want? Are they accredited? Is the school large or small, near or far from home, and is that what you want? What are their admissions requirements and can you meet them?

All of these questions must be answered as you select a school, and *before* you send off your application. Be practical about your selections, because most schools have a nonrefundable registration fee of from ten to twenty-five dollars. You don't want to send out lots of applications without thought, using a shotgun approach, assuming that the more you send out, the better your chances of getting accepted somewhere. Part of this reasoning is true, but you will also spend a lot more money than necessary and probably get accepted by many schools you don't want to attend.

Make your selection intelligently and send out no more than four or five applications. Send to your top three choices, then send one to a school that's not quite as competitive as the others, sort of a "safe" school. Also, send one to a school that's quite a bit out of your reach scholastically but one you'd give your eyeteeth to attend. Grades are not everything, and sometimes—just sometimes—you might have something in your background that such a school wants and it will accept you.

Having just gone through this with our own daughter, we are well qualified in the area of filling out applications. Be especially careful to give the admissions people exactly what they ask for on their form. Don't ad-lib. Don't send all sorts of stuff they didn't request. Don't decide not to send something they did request. Every school has its own requirements—honor them thoroughly and exactly.

Here is a supplement to the application for undergraduate admission to the Department of Architecture, University of Southern California. See how you would answer the questions. Decide on the materials you would send. Try to determine the impression they would make if you were the admissions officer. An exercise like this, early in the game, could make the difference between an acceptance or rejection from a favored school:

I. Please provide the following information, comprehensively but concisely, and preferably in your own handwriting. Use additional pages if necessary, and the back of this one.

    a) Describe your interest in Architecture, how that interest developed, and what you would like to do as an Architect. Include mention of any work experience or personal study you may have had which relates to the field.

    b) What are your special interests in addition to Architecture?

    c) Why do you think it is important that you attend the University at this time in your life?

    d) Do you understand the basic nature of the program offered by the USC Department of Architecture?

YES _____ NO _____

If the answer is NO, please describe the areas that are unclear and we will try to send you additional material related to your specific questions.

II. *Recommended*

Send to the Department of Architecture any examples (no more than four or five) of anything you have which shows how you perceive the world around you, which will give us an indication of how well you are able to communicate. Suitable material may include, for example, personal manuscripts, photographs, sketches, mechanical drawings, documentation of travel experiences, movies, etc. Submissions may not exceed the dimensions 8½" × 11". All submissions will be returned *only* if a self-addressed envelope, postage paid, is included.

43

With your schools selected and your applications sent out, you join tens of thousands of other high school students, and enter "nervous time"—a time of nail-biting, short tempers, and waiting for the mail each day.

4

SCHOOLING FOR FOUR, FIVE, OR SIX

Imagine—prestige schools actually recruiting women students! True, there are still schools that seem to embrace the old sexist ideas about college education. Although today they may do that embracing very quietly, they still do it. More aboveboard, and certainly much louder, are the words of schools actively looking for new women students.

In its booklet *A Place for Women,* Massachusetts Institute of Technology says:

"Why are so many more women now than ten years ago? The appeal of an education in science and technology is greater now. Active participation in our world now relies heavily on at least understanding the forces of science and technology that are on the crest of changes around us. We can do more than understand them; we can develop them, find new uses for them, and direct them toward solving some of the problems of our times.

"Career possibilities for women are also much greater now than ten years ago. The recent vigorous campaign by women to have their intellectual and creative talents recognized by the business and legislative communities is succeeding. Young women are changing their expectations; employers are promising equal opportunity, equal pay, and equal status.

"Why not be a doctor, engineer, architect, mathematician, chemist, lawyer, politician? These professions have always had some women, but a tiny fraction of the female population with

45

an aptitude for them. There are places for women as professionals in science, architecture, management, design, engineering, law, medicine, politics."

As you can understand, a great many architecture schools still are not waiting for you with open arms. Because of limited facilities and budgets, most schools of architecture (as most other professional colleges and universities) are very selective. In addition to your record of academic achievement in high school, they want even further assurance that the precious space each student takes up will be put to good use. They will check carefully to see that you show "reasonable promise for success in the program."

Now let's move past this point. You are in. You've made it. You are sitting on your bed in the dormitory of the school of your choice at the beginning of the fall term of your freshman year. What do the months and years ahead hold for you? What can you expect?

Start out by expecting a whole new ball game. The educational methods you knew in secondary school are a thing of the past. No longer will you concentrate on verbal and written skills. No longer will you use a slow, "spoon-fed" sequential learning system of moving, quite logically, from one bit of information to another in a carefully prescribed progression. No longer will you concentrate on verbal and written skills to the almost total exclusion of perceptual and visual skills.

Now you've got to develop the ability to handle a large amount of information and use it, not a bit at a time, but all at once. The very heart of architecture is the design process, a very complex problem-solving procedure in which you take an infinite number of important pieces of information in either language or mathematical terms and convert them into a series of forms using as many of the information pieces as possible.

If it sounds complicated, it is. There is nothing simple about the design process. True, today computers and other "state of the art advances" eliminate a considerable amount of "dog work," but plenty of information analysis and organization still remains in the architect's own hands and head.

Designing anything—especially when you are still learn-ing—requires hours and hours of problem-solving. Here it is taking place in a work space and course called a "studio"

Practicing architects have found and researchers agree that no matter how much design information gets organized, streamlined, or otherwise manipulated, at some point someone has to sit down and make architecture out of it—and that process is still called "design." As an architectural student, this will be your primary activity. And it's likely that the first time you jump in and try it you will get depressed and consider majoring in English literature instead. But designing, although a new mental activity to you, is something you *learn*, not inherit —and eventually it becomes as natural as walking (you had to learn that, too). Despite the frustration, anguish, and incredible complexity of the design process, it becomes enormously satisfying, and is great fun for those who develop the aptitude and skills involved. However, it ought to be pointed out at the start that for many persons designing always remains a foreign and painful process—as is evidenced by the high dropout rate in the first two years of many architecture schools.

The actual design process, at the learning stage, takes place in studios. In large, open, loft-like areas, you and other students, each with your own work space, will work out various architectural problems. Not only is the work space called a studio, but the course itself is known as "studio." You will continue taking studios throughout your architectural schooling. Since design uses as much information to solve problems as possible, you can understand that each design studio (or course) you take is more complicated and more challenging than the ones that preceded it. For example, your first design studio may start you out working on a simple single suburban or rural building project. Over a period of years, as your studios progress, you will probably end up working on very large, complex single- or multi-building projects in overcrowded urban situations.

But design is far from all of it. According to the ACSA: "Aside from design, which by your third undergraduate year is taking up half your time, you will also likely be taking courses in structures (one to two years), mechanical systems (usually one year), architectural history (one to two years), and lots of special electives and required courses that may include planning, graphics, crafts, computer programming, landscape architecture, materials, surveying, city planning, systems design, morphology (study of forms), industrialized building, environmental psychology, research methods, and architecture—some required and some electives. With the exception of only one or two schools, you will be in a university setting for several years, and that alone will affect you as much as the study of architecture will."

While you're up to your ears in architecture courses and everything else they toss at you, what about the added possible problems of discrimination? Will being a woman make college life tougher, easier, neither, or both? We have heard the comments and opinions of respected university professors who feel that times are changing for the better. What do the women have to say on the subject?

"I have felt largely that the discrimination I have encountered has been *valuable*—has *contributed* to my professional development. I have been required to outperform my male peers in order to do as well. The result is that I learned more than the average, acquired more skills at a faster rate because I was subtly 'pushed.' I can think of no valid reason why I should resent an attitude which has, in the end, been largely to my benefit, nor do I wish to change the attitude."

"At least they can't call women here dumb broads. And when there are more women at the Institute, and/or when a few gentle reminders are given to the chauvinist offenders, the offenses will probably disappear. Women, if a professor makes a sexist remark, tell him—he probably knows not what he does."

"If you're looking for equality, this is the place. Nobody is going to give you special treatment because you're a woman. If you want something, go work for it."

And here is a more in-depth look at the current situation in architecture schools from *Life Experiences in Environmental Design,* frank interviews with people who are studying architecture or have recently entered the field:

Graduate teaching associates prepare teaching material for a solar-heated community as part of their project assignments

"I have found that I have not had a great deal of problems that I realized, but there was a problem and I wasn't aware of it. And this was that I was viewed more or less as a female in architecture and not as a *real* student there. . . . The only time they would come over to see my design project was just to see what kind of bizarre solution this female had come up with this time. And they'd view it as a female solution; they wouldn't view it as an actual alternative. . . .

"To combat that, rather than get upset about it, I just played along with it. I just let them think what they wanted to and I never overtly tried to prove myself directly to any individual except perhaps the professor, because I wanted him to understand that I knew what I was doing. Generally, the professors were great, and they didn't view me just as a chick. They really got into what I was doing, and I have no hard feelings about how any of the professors treated me because I was a female. The students were really incredibly nasty at times. They didn't want to respect me as a designer, and not until my junior year did they really understand that I could do things. I will never forget a major breakthrough when one day we were working on a big center that had a large site plan involved with it, and it needed a lot of parking. I was roaming around another studio, and I was talking to a guy whom I'd known very well since my freshman year. We were really good buddies, but he'd never come over and critiqued my designs and he never knew what I was doing. So I went down to critique his design, and I looked at it and I said, 'This doesn't work at all.' So I got the tracing paper and I just went through the whole thing with him and explained to him why his was so out of range. It just didn't work in terms of circulation flow, in terms of view, in terms of orientation; there were just an awful lot of things that he had overlooked that seemed to me to be the major basis of the plot plan. And he was appalled; he was absolutely amazed that I could *think* and that I could come down and critique his design and actually know what I was talking about. And he came to respect me, and gradually all his buddies and the rest of the class decided that I really did know what I was doing. And after that time, they'd come down, and they'd help me out, they'd come over to my studio and they'd say, 'Hey, we gotta check out what Peterson's doing now.' And so they'd critique me just as I did them. But it really took a lot. There're still probably 50% of the guys in the class who will not come over to my desk and actually critique what I have. Either they're afraid that I'm going to break, that I'm not going to be able to handle the criticism, or that I won't even understand what they're saying."

You may not agree with the way other women have handled the question of prejudice or discrimination, but you have seen that it *does* exist, and there are probably as many ways to deal with it as there are women architecture students.

51

And so, by now, you see that it won't be easy. But, frankly, it's not easy for male students either. Architecture is not a "snap" career course. Keeping that in mind will help you as it has thousands of other men and women who wanted careers in architecture badly enough.

One of the major choices to be made is "Should it be a four-, five-, or six-year course?" What's the difference and how will they cram all the courses, all the studios, and all the information and practical work into those years?

Just about all the schools can be divided into two different formats. The first is the more traditional one, a five-year program culminating in a Bachelor of Architecture as the first professional degree.

In the traditional schools, you enter the architecture program directly. The curriculum is structured, yet flexible enough to allow room for you to choose your own elective courses. Some schools will offer two or three (or more) basic "cores," allowing you to focus on one particular design, management, or technology area of architecture. These five-year programs generally relate to today's expanded practice roles. If you think that is what you know, and that is what you'll want, the five-year program is the most direct way of getting there.

The other format is a bit more flexible, allows for more options, and is especially suited for students who think they want architecture, but aren't 100 percent positive. This six-year program leads to a Master of Architecture as the first professional degree, and gives you the opportunity to be in architecture while checking out some other possibilities.

This sort of program is made possible by what is called a "2 + 2 + 2" format. Simply stated, it means that the first two years are spent taking care of the general requirements of your school as well as the basic introductory architecture courses. The next two years give you the fundamentals of architecture, usually mixed with exposure to environmental design courses. At the end of these four years, at most schools, you will receive a nonprofessional bachelor's degree in art, science, or environmental design.

The two graduate years are usually quite wide open, allowing you a fascinating variety of in-depth options in either professional or research areas. There is lots of room to choose from courses designed for immediate use in the world of architecture or from research programs that relate architecture to many other fields. At the end of those two years you should receive your Master of Architecture degree.

If you think that at this point you will be ready to go out and

UNIVERSITY OF TEXAS, ARLINGTON

Design class, guided by an award-winning interior designer, prepare plans for the interiors of a complex, multi-unit housing project for a suburban area

start building buildings, large or small, hold it . . . not just yet. You still have a long way to go. At least three years of internship await you before you are allowed to take the registration exam. As you may suddenly now realize, internship is just as important for architects as it is for doctors.

It's important not only because it is required for taking the registration exam, but because it gives you a chance to get real-world experience and develop the judgment and sense of responsibility that are the marks of a professional of any kind. Through internship, you will have the opportunity to develop that important habit of continued learning. For an architect, learning must be a lifelong process that does not stop at the end of the formal education period. This education will help you round out and expand information and knowledge you'll need to practice architecture.

Now, about that registration. Is there only one road to that ultimate goal? Does the route to registration have to be accredited school of architecture plus internship plus licensing exam? Although that is not always the only way, it does seem to make the most sense for someone who is about to start out on this long road.

Accredited schools, unaccredited schools, work experience, Equivalency Exam, Professional Exam—are all part of the recipe to create a registered architect. Here's how it works out. The National Council of Architectural Registration Boards (NCARB) prepares two, long, comprehensive exams. The Equivalency Exam is for everyone who does not have an architecture degree from an NAAB-accredited school. Passing this exam qualifies you to take the Professional Exam.

To take the Professional Exam you must be at least twenty-one, hold an accredited first professional degree in architecture, and have three years' experience. There are various combinations of requirements to take the Equivalency Exam. Many states and architectural jurisdictions have their own requirements, so when the time comes, checking with your own State Registration Board is imperative. For example, the State of California works it out this way:

A full eight years of study and/or work experience is necessary before licensing. Credit toward this eight-year requirement is granted after the State Board reviews academic transcripts according to the following scale:

At accredited schools of architecture:

B. Arch. plus accredited M. Arch. = 6 years of educational credit can apply immediately for Equivalency Exam.

B.S. in Arch. plus accredited M. Arch. = 5 years of educational credit can apply immediately for Equivalency Exam.

B. Arch. = 5 years of educational credit can apply immediately for Equivalency Exam.

B.S. in Arch. = 3.5 years of educational credit can apply for Equivalency Exam after 1.5 years of experience.

At unaccredited schools of architecture:

M. Arch. = 4.5 years of educational credit can apply for Equivalency Exam after .5 years of experience.

B.S. in Arch. = 3.5 years of educational credit can apply for Equivalency Exam after 1.5 years of experience.

Because architects are involved with the health, safety, and welfare of people, the exams are complete, difficult, and long. The AIA itself admits that the Professional Exam is tough. It is a two-day, four-part exam that is graded by machines. Either you pass it or you don't.

Looking at the exam a little more closely, we see that it is a standard exam prepared by the NCARB, and although the same exam is used in every state, only the state in which you take it can grant your registration. Through NCARB, however, you can gain reciprocity—that is, you can obtain a license in other states because you had the right preliminary education

Women and men work on an equal basis in many schools where the feeling is strong that "nobody gets special treatment. If you want something, go work for it"

and experience qualifications, and because you passed the exam and received the license in the first state. States have reciprocal agreements through NCARB, so you don't have to worry about spending your entire professional life taking registration exams.

The exam doesn't waste its time testing academic knowledge. NCARB assumes you have all that necessary knowledge if you have received an accredited architecture degree. Rather, the Professional Exam tests your ability to put your knowledge and professional training to work and actually make decisions.

This two-day exam is given in four sessions totaling sixteen hours. The specific areas covered in the four sessions are: environmental analysis, building programming, design and technology, and construction. You are tested on your ability to make strategic decisions on major environmental issues or projects; to synthesize basic general knowledge; to exercise environmental value judgment; to understand the architect's responsibilities to the public, the client, and the profession.

The Equivalency Exam, unlike the Professional Exam, is a test of technical and academic knowledge. It is given in three parts over two days in twenty-four hours of evaluation. It consists of Part I—History and Theory of Architecture and Environmental Planning; Part II—Architectural Design and Site Planning; and Part III—Construction Theory and Practice. Two parts are machine-graded. One grade, Pass or Fail, is given for each multiple-choice section of the examination. The other part, the design/site examination, is a graphic problem and will be graded by the State Board which administers this examination.

Exams complete, you are on your way, with diploma, registration certificate, and loads of information and ideas—ready and available, waiting to burst forth and make the world a better place to live. Long hours and hard work are still ahead of you, but so also are the rewards and the satisfaction you waited and worked so long to attain.

5

LOTS OF WAYS TO SPECIALIZE

The time has come. Somewhere along the way you've got to make a decision. You've been standing with your nose pressed against the candy store window long enough. Throughout your college career you've seen all sorts of courses that lead to all sorts of degrees and then to all sorts of jobs. Many of them look so good to you, making a decision becomes almost impossible. But decide you must. One way or the other—you've either got to pick your specialty or decide not to specialize.

To make matters even more difficult in the specialization department, there are really two different kinds of specialization in the field of architecture. Some architects, especially those in private practice, specialize in individual kinds of buildings; for example, they become "experts" in shopping centers, libraries, homes, hospitals, or firehouses. Some cut it so fine as to specialize in one particular kind of building rather than another similar type—for instance, synagogues rather than churches. Still others concentrate on buildings with very specialized internal functions, like cafeterias, diagnostic centers, and laboratories.

And then there are the specialties that are related, but are more like close cousins than brothers and sisters. Included in this list, but not limited to those listed, are such areas as environmental design, architectural engineering, construction engineering, industrial design, interior design, building science, building construction, and city and regional planning.

A few ground rules are important for you to know so your decision-making can become more meaningful. First, all of these areas are open and available to anyone who is interested and capable—women *and* men. Don't allow yourself to be put off by stories from construction workers or anyone else. If a certain kind of work appeals to you and you want it for your life's work, go after it.

Second, there are no definitive answers to questions of suitability. For which specialties are women best suited? Women are best suited for the kind of work they like and do best, and that is pretty much the way men approach their career choices. There has always been the attitude on the part of male architects that women are "best suited" for careers in interior design, programming, graphics, etc., and that men "belong" in the construction areas. This kind of self-serving chauvinism is best answered by the architect who said, "I consider myself an architect. I am not a woman architect. I am an architect, and as a qualified architect, I can do everything and anything related to my work from the lowest to the highest level."

Third, your decision to specialize is made during your schooling and carried out within it; you need not complete your program and then return or go on to specialize, as you would in medicine. All the specialties listed are contained within curricula designed to be as complete as possible, usually including practical experience, leading to a degree within five or six years. Some programs require a B.Arch. as a first professional degree and add the Master's later. Others run the entire course through and award a single degree (usually a Master's) on completion. Whichever specialty you choose, you can be sure that whatever courses you take or whatever road you follow, there will be little if any "waste" in case of a change of mind.

It's a good idea to find out as much as you can about each of the architecture specialties, so you should sample a course here or there, and aim yourself in the right direction for you and your future. The specialties listed here contain only basic descriptions of the courses required. They are meant to whet your appetite. Full investigation to complete the meal is up to you.

BUILDING CONSTRUCTION

Architectural engineering emphasizes the scientific and engineering aspects of the planning, design, and construction of buildings. Majoring in this field will give you the fundamentals of engineering leading to private practice as a professional engineer, to employment as an architectural engineer, to facilities-coordination positions, to public service, or to other positions requiring a knowledge of engineering design, construction, and maintenance of buildings.

The specific area of building science emphasizes building construction engineering and construction management.

Courses that should be taken include architectural engineering, chemistry, calculus, composition and rhetoric, computer graphics, the writing of ideas, general physics, matrices and statistics, architectural electives, working drawings, environmental engineering, architectural acoustics, strength of materials, dynamics, building construction assemblies, industrial accounts, building cost analysis, soils engineering, surveying, personnel administration, foundation engineering, and site engineering fundamentals.

BUILDING SCIENCE

Graduates with degrees in building science will become the managers in the construction industry. The course involves studies in the design of structural and mechanical systems for buildings, construction procedures, building cost estimation, and construction management.

The curriculum requires a broad general knowledge of a variety of subject areas. They include English composition, geometry and calculus, technology and civilization, materials and construction, economics, accounting, history of building, computer programming, strength of materials, construction prob-

Checking the minutest details on a cold Sunday morning before "opening day" is more pleasure than chore for this architect who specializes in suburban library/media centers

lems, technical writing, industrial relations, architecture and design, legal aspects of engineering, construction methods and estimating, building equipment, and other technical electives.

CONSTRUCTION ENGINEERING

The graduate construction engineer will be expert in construction planning and scheduling, management, materials procurement, equipment selection, and cost control. As a professional construction engineer, she must have a strong fundamental knowledge of both engineering and management principles, as well as sound training in business procedures, economics, and human behavior.

The construction engineer's training blends three areas: building, heavy construction, and mechanical construction.

Courses include materials and methods of building construction, construction contract, documents and specifications, construction cost estimating, planning construction of institutions, real estate finance, heavy construction equipment and methods, construction organization and management (insurance, bonding, financial records, financial policies, labor relations, and pertinent labor legislation), concrete construction and formwork design, construction planning and scheduling and case studies.

CITY AND REGIONAL PLANNING

The creation of better living environments is one of the nation's most urgent tasks. In our cities, where pollution, congestion, and poverty are inhibiting the healthy growth of those cities and their inhabitants, proper planning for change is essential.

City and regional planning, a relatively new profession, is one answer to many modern problems. Its central focus is the physical environment of cities and regions, the forces that shape this environment, the plans and policies possible to ease and eliminate urban and regional problems, the available governmental and private resources, and the way solutions may be implemented. The purpose of city planning is to integrate the physical, social, economic, and political aspects of community development in finding solutions to urban and regional problems.

Graduates of professional programs in regional planning are prepared for careers in city, county, metropolitan, regional, state, and federal agencies. They may also work through community or citizens groups, or with private organizations that deal with such varied problems as housing, poverty, human resources development, transportation, urban renewal, and regional development.

Courses include planning techniques, transportation for city planners, case studies in urban development, housing, regional landscape analysis, human resources planning, and federal community assistance programs.

URBAN PLANNING

Urban planners contribute their knowledge, skills, and human understanding to improving the quality of life in urban society. The field is concerned with those aspects of planning which deal directly or indirectly with the quality of the urban environment, access to opportunity in the urban setting, and availability of urban services. Planning is both technical and political, so the urban planner must acquire competence in both areas, becoming a technical expert, public servant, and facilitator as well as a creative leader.

To be able to do all these things, you as an urban planner must be trained to understand the theory of economic, social, political, and physical processes of urban society. You must also be able to apply these skills to the solution of current urban problems.

A degree in urban planning requires such courses as the city as a political system, the city as an economic system, introduction to computer applications, housing in the suburbs, urban transportation planning, land use survey and modeling, planning and programming of correctional facilities, and needs assessment.

INTERIOR DESIGN

Interior designers involve themselves with people in all of their living conditions: work—offices, shops, factories; recreation—hotels, theaters; services—hospitals, institutions; home; and others. The interior designer does research, design, and specification work in such areas as lighting systems, furnishings, and equipment.

This involvement in the design of interior space makes the interior designer a coordinator of social, historical, and technical elements with space, surface, and material.

Although the description sounds technical, a look at the courses that are included in this program should allay any fears —history of world art, geometry and calculus, history and technology in architecture, principles of management, contemporary interiors, technical writing, creative crafts (textile design, weaving, or photography), and electives in the natural sciences. This combination indicates the broad background the interior designer needs to provide the right answers to the unique problems of her field.

URBAN DESIGN

Urban design is meant to serve the public interest. Its goal is to serve as many people as possible rather than just the client and the people who will directly use the building and/or its space. The urban designer provides a solution to design problems that not only satisfies single-purpose vested interests but also provides benefits beyond those interests.

The urban designer meshes the physical elements of the built environment with people and functions around it.

Urban design connects budgetary, legislative, political, and physical events that take place over a period of time. Although urban designers do not design buildings, maintain facilities, or share in the profits, they must be sensitive to all these concerns.

Elements of politics, transportation, housing, education, community services, economic feasibility, and environmental

UNIVERSITY OF TEXAS, ARLINGTON

Students specializing in interior design are thrilled to actually use the chair and sofa they designed and constructed for class projects

implications are included in the urban designer's research, analysis, and ultimate design. The work of the urban designer is intended to serve as a guide to decision-making groups, including citizens and government, assisting them in projecting a future urban environment that will affect the entire community.

A design studio student's model is critiqued by an architect and another student before the finishing touches are added

Courses in law, finance, development, implications of politics and urban policy, and management are included in the urban design curriculum.

INDUSTRIAL DESIGN

Industrial designers are concerned with the practical and aesthetic relation of products and systems to those who use them. The industrial designer is a member of the research and development team and is responsible for the product's shape, color, proportion, and texture. She is deeply concerned with such factors of use as efficiency, convenience, safety, comfort, maintenance, and cost.

The industrial designer is often skilled in drafting, model making, photography, and sketching.

No matter what the product may be, the industrial designer is concerned with the well-being of both the individual consumer and the community. She must be familiar with the materials and production techniques of modern industry and aware of the importance of the forms she gives to everyday objects as reflections of current times and culture.

The activities of the industrial designer extend into product design, packaging, graphics, display, company identification, transportation, and furniture as well as specialized architecture.

The student specializing in industrial design is introduced to such courses as design methods, product planning, visual statistics, materials, manufacturing methods, consumer psychology, and environmental studies.

Other courses include technology and civilization, woodworking, welding science, sheet-metal design, technical illustration, gauges and measures, principles of marketing, industrial psychology, human factors, and industrial sociology.

6

REAL CAREERS FOR REAL PEOPLE

Everything is quiet, calm, and serene. Light is beginning to filter through the slats of the venetian blinds. It's the beginning of what will be a busy day, and since most of their days are like that, the family savors the waking and starts out nice and slow.

The creative juices start stirring first. This two-architect, two-child family is still in bed. The wife twists a bit and opens one eye to squint at the numbers on the digital clock beside the bed. Still plenty of time to get up, get everything done, and get to the office by 9:00.

Yesterday had been an unusually long, hard, strength-sapping but rewarding day. She smiles, remembering the comment of her son, years ago when he was five. Asked what he wanted to be, he thought a moment, then said, "I think I want to be a doctor so I can take care of you poor architects who work so long and hard."

On the other side of the bed, her husband was smiling too. He was thinking of yesterday and what they had accomplished. They had met their deadline and done it calmly and coolly—well, reasonably calmly and coolly. They had worked long into the night to get what they wanted, and they had gotten it finished. And they were satisfied with their work. For them, work under pressure was their best kind of work—the creative "yeast" flowed best then. When they were not working under pressure, they thought more in concepts, enjoying the creativity, adapting, making changes, having a good time, but not really making anything jell.

She moved slightly, which caused him to turn and find her staring at him. They were amused to note that they were both smiling and, as married couples who are "tuned in" so often do, each knew exactly what the other was smiling about.

These are the opening moments in the daily love story of real people. They love each other and their life. They love their home, their family, and their work. Whether they are typical or not, we really don't know. Who among us can say who or what is typical? But they certainly are crackerjack architects and incredibly nice people, so why not tell their story?

Let's follow a day in the life of a successful architect, wife, mother, and human being. Let's follow along as she "decides to get started."

Action starts as everyone leaves bed (with varying degrees of groaning), wanders into bathrooms, into closets, and finally into clothes. For a while it resembles an old Marx Brothers movie as the family members, ignoring each other except for a few garbled words as they pass in the hall, move in and out of doors and rooms. First meetings are pajama-clad, then partially dressed, and finally, downstairs, fully dressed.

Paul, fifteen, is first into the kitchen, knows exactly what he has to do in this choreographed breakfast, and does it. Pam is twelve, and knows exactly what she is to do (but rarely does it). She is a master of the stall tactic, speaking first to one member of the family, then another, until her mother has completed all her own jobs and Pam's as well.

Mom and Dad work hand in hand at everything, breakfast included. She says, "With four hands, everything takes half the time." It wasn't always like that. As a matter of fact, until very recently Dad did a lot of standing around, asking what he could do, and actually did very little.

"About three years ago," she recalls, "I wanted the kids to know that not only women make the meals and clean up after them. The idea was to have a completely liberated household. So we made an agreement. One week I would do all the cooking and all the washing and the next week my husband would do all the cooking and all the washing.

"We started our liberated meal program and after about three weeks our daughter said to me, 'Why is it that when Daddy does the cooking you're in there helping him, but when you're doing it he's sitting down reading the paper?' That ended that, and now we use the four-handed approach."

With breakfast and cleanup completed, the in-one-door-out-the-other routine is repeated as everyone prepares to leave the house. The children head for their bus stops, one off to the

FENTEN

A partner in an architectural firm works with contractors on a job site. She collects a list of questions to be answered later, after study back at the office

junior high, the other to the high school. The partners head for their car and the short ride to their office in the center of a small, upper-middle-income suburban town. There's not much talking in the car as they listen to the news, weather, and sports on the radio.

It's just a few minutes after nine when they arrive at the office. A quick check reveals few changes since they left late the previous night. The drafts men and women are working on the revised plans for a synagogue/catering hall/youth center complex that must be presented to a board of directors within two days. Each of the partners works with the people on the drafting tables for a few minutes, and then, convinced that everything is moving along smoothly, they get back into the car to visit one of their "children," a large student union building on a nearby college campus.

They are planning to use the same exterior materials on their new synagogue as they used on their student union building and they want to see, firsthand, once again, how they weather, if they age well, and, generally, if they have lived up to the expectations of the architect and the client. After a long, slow, deliberate walk around the outside of the building, they move inside. They drift along, slowly, with a group of students—looking, checking, touching.

They find themselves behind a man and two women who are chatting as they walk. One woman turns to the other and says, "You know, whoever designed this building must have selected the plates, tableware, and cutlery used in the cafeteria. They just had to have been selected by the same person—there's a look, a feeling about everything."

The two architects turn toward each other, beaming. After a few seconds' hesitation, the male partner steps in front of the people and reaches out to shake hands with the woman who had just spoken. The woman, startled, asks why he wants to shake her hand—"What have I won, or done?"

She is quite surprised to hear him answer, "We are the architects of this building, and I don't know how you knew it —but we *did* select all the things here. All the china, cutlery,

71

glassware, everything. We even designed the logo for the building and then adapted it for the china."

They all continue chatting for a while and then go their separate ways. Although many architects do not provide this complete and total service, this team does. They feel that "everything associated with a building has to fit in with the building. All the pieces must fit together to make a beautiful, useful whole. Under our supervision the landscaping is done, furnishings are selected, and everything else is chosen and installed under our watchful eyes and, often, helping hands. We even help the client go out for bids to assure that the client gets the best value per dollar. To us, every part of the job is all in a day's work."

Delighted with the encounter and their most current reappraisal of "their" student union building, the architects leave the building, get into their car and return to the office just in time for lunch.

Back in the office, sharing a desk and the sandwiches they have brought from home, they talk about their inspection trip.

This trip has been a break in their usual routine of "job trips" each Wednesday. The trips are usually shared by the partners and two other members of their staff, each one going out on a weekly trip. On occasion, it doesn't work out that way, as one client may relate particularly well to one member of the group; in that case, that member will conduct all meetings with the client.

The partners usually figure on at least four or five hours for an inspection trip, making it an "all-day affair." The partner who goes meets with all the contractors, checks all the specifications, and brings back a list of questions that couldn't be answered at the job site. No matter what else they "have cooking" the partners personally visit all their job sites at least once each month.

Discussion over lunch continues with thoughts and progress checks on jobs currently under way, how designs might be improved on others, what has been done on one job and what they would like to do about another. They plan and review as

No detail is too small for the architect designer as she makes careful inspection at one of her job sites. She knows what to look for and where trouble spots are likely to appear

73

the sandwiches disappear. They linger, talk, and work quietly, pleasantly. There is no bolting down of food—and, happily, unless there is an emergency, no telephone interruption. Both architects consider this a combination working, pleasure, and relaxing period. They love what they are doing and enjoy talking about various facets of the several jobs on which they are working.

She has always believed "that the ideal situation in an architectural firm is to have one job in design, one job ready for bid, and one job under construction. It can get kind of boring if all your jobs are in the same stage at the same time." Their conversations and reviews are designed to keep their approach fresh and the various jobs moving along at just the right speed, with progress constantly being surveyed and double-checked.

Crumbled aluminum foil and empty soft drink cans are tossed into wastebaskets, officially closing the lunch period. Each architect goes to a specific location: desk, drafting table, model, and picks up where he or she left off. Each may do some designing, some sketching, or some question-answering about jobs they have under construction. They are in and out of each other's areas to confer on various details as they develop, so solutions can be refined before they are committed to paper.

This is the afternoon the "library people" are coming. The architects have been told of the committee's desire for a new library/meeting room/reference center building. Today they will be asked to present their initial proposal for the building. Considerable time and effort have gone into the preparations for this presentation. It all started about a month ago when the phone rang just after lunch.

"You never really know what the next day or the next job will be. That's a great part of the fun of this business. Anyway, a man called and said, 'We'd like you to design a new library center for us.' Our immediate question was to determine where he had heard of us. Who recommended us? Did the committee get our name from friends? Were we recommended by a former client? Did they find us in the Yellow Pages?

FENTEN

On inspection trips, deliberately scheduled for the weekend, this architect often invites her children to come along. She says they "frequently come up with some fantastic observations"

"If they know our work, it's one thing," she explained, "but if they picked us out of the Yellow Pages, a whole different approach must be used. Often, these people have no idea what an architect does, nor the services we provide. We have to educate them generally about our profession and specifically about our company.

"Sometimes the prospective client becomes an ex-prospective client. That happens when the client says, 'We know what we want, we just want someone to draw it.' Our answer is always a very courteous, 'Thanks—but no, thanks.' We are not interested in doing that kind of work. We're not certain what these people want, but we are pretty sure they don't want architects."

Today, the "library people," having gotten past step one, are ready for step two, the architect's presentation. The time between the initial contact and today's presentation has been spent researching the kind of building the client wants and needs. Since the architects have done large libraries before, the amount of research is just a bit less than usual. Since the site of the new building has already been chosen, the architects have visited it, checked the surrounding area, looked at access roads, and mentally placed their new building on the client's site. With all of this research completed and sketches on hand, they are ready for the meeting.

Promptly at 3:00 P.M. the library building committee arrive. They are welcomed into the conference room, and after brief but cordial greetings, the lights are dimmed and the architects present a slide show of some of their previous jobs. The slides appear on the screen for just a moment, because usually the client is not interested in someone else's building, but in what the architect has done for *this* job.

The architect explains, "We are showing you these slides so you have a better idea of the kind of work we do. If you don't like what you have seen on the slides, there is no point in going any farther. Of course, your building will be designed especially for you, but it is important that you know what our completed buildings look like."

There is a lot of nodding of the heads of the library committee members. The architects then give their proposal for the building, zeroing in specifically on how it takes care of the special problems previously presented by the committee. The architect partners speak in turn, and it quickly becomes obvious to the library committee that they have done this many times before. When they have completed their presentation, they answer all the questions from the committee.

The committee members seem pleased with what they have seen and heard. They chat among themselves as they smile, rise, and prepare to leave. "There's just one more thing," the architect says, stopping cold the chatting and moving. "You all must agree to becoming very involved in the work on this building. After all, it will be a reflection of what you and your community need and want. All the decisions will be yours. We'll recommend, but *you'll* decide."

Even more delighted than before, the committee members ask just a few more questions, leave a list of home and business phone numbers, and are ushered to the door. The architects each take a deep breath before shaking hands firmly and quickly, and finishing off with a brief, tight hug. Then each heads for a different end of the office.

They are nearing the end of another long, hard, varied, and rewarding day. After some cleaning up and detail work, they head for car and family. It will be their usual and preferred kind of evening; a long, pleasant dinner, planned by Mom, started by the kids, and finished by all, plenty of conversation covering the entire day, some TV, perhaps a little reading, then off to bed. "We are not very active socially. It's too much like hard work for us. We don't especially like social engagements or dinner invitations. They're just too time-consuming. If we have to sit in a room and make small talk for three or four hours, it becomes a drag. It's especially difficult because I keep thinking of the other things I could and would prefer to be doing.

"Besides, it wouldn't be fair to our children. We like to be with them and they seem to enjoy being with us, so why give all this up for other people? On most afternoons, Pam comes straight from school to the office and does her homework (at any empty drafting table—she thinks that's 'cool') while we are working. We meet Paul at home and then all pitch in to finish dinner preparations. We have fun together because we all have a stake in everything. It's great. When we go on inspection trips over the weekends, the children go along and frequently come up with some fantastic observations. They seem to see things that all the adults miss. And they have a fine time. We can tell. It's not a command performance—we offer them the opportunity to come along and they very rarely refuse. It's truly a pleasure when everyone's interested in everyone else. Makes it a lot easier and a lot more pleasant to be doing what I love —to be an architect, wife, and mother and not have regrets about any of these careers."

7

JOBS IN RELATED FIELDS

Your interest in architecture is what led you to pick up and read this book. If you have read this far, you have gotten a better idea of what architecture is all about. One of the things you have not learned is which of the many architectural paths you'd like to try first. We say "first" because life is often a surprising thing. You can be so sure of something one day, unsure the next, and positive you don't want that thing the day after that.

Spending a great deal of time, energy, and money for an education and then discovering you may have been educated for the wrong thing is a miserable experience. How much better it is to learn as much as you can about a general career choice, read and discover all the avenues open to you in that profession, choose one or two, then move along with your eyes and mind wide open to the possibilities.

Consider the kind of person you are, how you like to spend your time, what you find fun, your strong points, your weaknesses—then see if there isn't a specialty that fits you just right.

Para-professional—These are careers in the field of architecture that do not require professional licensing or a degree from an accredited school. They are classified under the umbrella terms of drafting, graphic arts, and administration.

Though they are para-professional areas of practice, they are frequently pursued by qualified registered architects because of specialized interests or skills. Courses in these areas are offered by many junior, community, and technical colleges in two-year curricula. This is often a good beginning for students who are not too crazy about school and feel that two more years will be enough; didn't do too well in high school and can use the two years to pull their grades up; feel that the training given in two years is all they want or will need; have financial problems that keep them from going to a four-year college. There are probably as many more reasons as there are students. The two-year course is also a good place to "get your feet wet" if you are not positive that architecture is for you. If the answer turns out to be yes, you can always transfer to a four-year school.

The AIA describes the programs developed for these two-year curricula for these career areas:

1. Drafting, Specifications, Estimating Sequence. This requires:

     Understanding
        —of the architectural and design professions and segments of the building industry;
        —of the design and production process in architecture;
        —of the basic mathematical and physical factors.
     Knowledge
        —of building materials, systems, and construction, together with the legal and practical standards affecting them.
     Skills
        —in verbal and graphic communication associated with technical drawings and documents.

2. Graphic Arts, Models, Reproduction Sequence. This requires:

     Understanding
        —of the architectural and design professions and other components of the building industry;

—of the design and production process in architecture;

—of basic mathematics.

Knowledge

—of visual and graphic communication and interpretation of technical drawings and instruction.

Skills

—in layout and production of two- and three-dimensional models and charts;

—in operation of reproduction techniques.

3. Administration, Data Processing, Information Sequence. This requires:

Understanding

—of the architectural and design profession and of business organization and procedures;

—of business and data processing mathematics.

Knowledge

—of the language, programming, and potentials of the computer, data processing, and information systems.

Skills

—in operation of machines, computers, and devices in contemporary business and architectural practice.

Government—About 10 percent of the country's licensed architects work for government on local, state, federal, or international levels. Being a government architect may not have occurred to you, but it is a possibility not to overlook.

Describing its work as not being terribly different from working for anyone else in the field, the government suggests that federal agencies have the same kinds of design problems that design offices have anywhere—"only more of them": Sometimes government functions as the client, sometimes as the designer, sometimes as both. Agency offices are organized in a variety of ways. Some agencies have specialists; some, generalists. Some have large, very structured design offices; some have smaller, less formal ones. The kinds of projects and the extent of your involvement in them vary a great deal, depending on where you work.

"As an architect you could assist in the design of an office building, help to program the design of a hospital, or work on the development of housing standards.

"Depending on your experience, knowledge, and capabilities, you might be working 'on the board' or managing a team dealing with multimillion-dollar projects.

"Of course, all the assignments are not equally exciting. There is the usual share of shop drawings, schedules, and paperwork, too. But a lot of the work is a real challenge, and the scope and sheer number of federal programs offer a unique opportunity for constructive work and professional growth.

"Applicants must have successfully completed a curriculum in an accredited college or university leading to a bachelor's degree in architecture or architectural engineering.

"For each year short of graduation, a candidate lacking a degree must have one year of experience in an architect's office or in architectural work of such character and diversity as to be a satisfactory substitute for the required education. In the absence of college courses, five years of such experience is required. This experience must demonstrate a thorough knowledge of the fundamental principles and theories of professional architecture and an understanding of the field of architecture comparable to that which would have been acquired through the successful completion of a full four-year curriculum.

"State registration to practice architecture may be substituted as fully meeting the basic education and experience requirements.

"Architects will be rated on their technical knowledge and skills, ability to control and order their work, to research their work thoroughly, and to communicate orally and in writing."

Landscape architecture—This field seems much more interested in attracting women than do others. The American Society of Landscape Architects (ASLA), founded over seventy-

THE OHIO STATE UNIVERSITY

Though the number of women teachers in architecture lags behind other disciplines, progress is being made as many schools start talented people as graduate teaching associates

five years ago by seven men and Beatrix Jones Farrand, who, among other things, designed the gardens at Dumbarton Oaks, has always encouraged women to enter the profession. It now has an ongoing program to show even more women the opportunities for meaningful careers in landscape architecture.

There are some basic differences between landscape architecture and other architectural specialties. In the other specialties, such as engineering, interior design, and city planning, practitioners deal with people and their *constructed* environments. Landscape architecture is more fundamental, centering around the relationships between people and their *natural* environment.

Defining its work, the ASLA says, "The landscape architect must look at the environment as a whole and must understand the scale and properties of regional, community, and neighborhood landscapes as total complexes of constructed and natural elements, not as distinct and unrelated parts.

"The landscape architect may be called upon to design a residential garden, locate a scenic parkway, establish a community tree-planting program, propose a university expansion master plan, or prepare reports for land use for an entire geographic area. In other instances we find landscape architects developing the site plan and supervising the construction of a downtown mall, an industrial park, a golf course, school grounds, or a trailer park. Today, as the country and the world recognize the need to preserve and protect our natural resources, the work that landscape architects have been doing with respect to natural resources planning becomes of primary importance. Each project must be designed to fulfill human needs in a civilized world. Each must be designed for optimum use today—and tomorrow."

To give us a better idea of the field and how women are practicing successfully in it, the ASLA has given us some of the following examples:

". . . a principal owner of an East Coast landscape architectural firm employing both men and women which specializes in recreation and park design who says: 'I would like to encourage more first-rate minds to become landscape architects. I suspect lots of them are women.'

". . . a designer with a state highway department who switched from landscape architectural aspects of highway design to engineering work because she found it more interesting.

". . . an employee of a private office who has designed a memorial park at the U.S. Coast Guard Academy as well as college planning projects who wished that more women would enter the profession because . . . 'in this era of environmental concern, women could contribute greatly to what landscape architecture is all about—the proper balance between nature and progress.'

". . . a woman who not only runs her own office, but also lectures, does horticultural consulting, and has recently written a book on plant materials for use in urban areas.

". . . an educator actively involved in endeavoring to increase the number of women in landscape architectural education.

". . . an employee of a municipal transportation authority who is concerned with the creation of environmental quality on already disturbed sites such as airports.

". . . a government employee who has prepared site development plans for various Western park facilities."

Code enforcement—Another field of architecture actively "going out" after women to counteract what they call "a great deal of sexism in this field" is code enforcement. There are no reasons why women cannot become building inspectors to enforce building, plumbing, heating, and electrical fire prevention codes. Currently there are a "few dozen women building inspectors, but no administrators." However, women *are* engaged in teaching building officials.

To become a building inspector does not require any great physical strength. The person should like to be outside a great deal, both winter and summer, and be able to drive a car in all sorts of weather. Inspectors are usually trained within the building department itself, learning such things as the use of the performance code, permit insurance and follow-up, plan reading, height and area limitations, basic construction inspection for one- and two-family dwellings, and inspection report writing. Few colleges or universities offer full courses of training for this field.

Building officials learn how to work with the public, how to enforce the code regulations, how to read plans, how to issue permits, how to inspect buildings, how to write inspection reports, how to issue violation notices, etc. They may also learn a great deal about municipal zoning, since this is an integral part of any inspector's duties.

Being an effective building official requires that the woman realize she is a law enforcement officer and is duty-bound to uphold the code regulations. An inspector makes many inspections each day. This means she must talk to many people and issue violation notices no matter who says or does what, and she must know how to file reports and follow through on all inspections.

Another field now open to women is that of plan reviewer. Usually these women are engineers or architects who check plans for code compliance. These women work exclusively with the code and must be trained in the use, interpretation, and applications of it. A small building department would only have one inspector who will function as inspector, zoning examiner, and plan reviewer. However, larger building departments have a plan review section. This job is ideal for women who can pay close attention to detail, have technical minds, and enjoy working in law enforcement.

Other related careers—There are many other career fields open to you if you are interested in architecture and have the proper educational background. Sample some of the following career suggestions and see if they might fit into your career planning.

One of the biggest gripes of architects, and indeed of all creative people, is that their critics are frequently unqualified by most standards to make critical comments. To paraphrase an old saying, the architect's contention is that "those who can, do, and those who can't, criticize."

Many newspapers, magazines, and TV stations regularly carry critical or explanatory stories by architectural journalists and critics. As we become more and more concerned about the world we live, work, and play in, the opportunities for educated and experienced writers, trained and knowledgeable in this field, will expand. Add to that the fascinating area of architectural photography and you have careers that shouldn't be overlooked by women or men.

Almost all construction requires loan money. As a result, architects interested in finance and construction economics can find many positions open with banks, insurance companies, government agencies, and stock exchange brokerages. Couple that with the idea that many public institutions finance construction through taxes and special bond issues, and you find additional career opportunities for architects who are well versed in public finance and tax administration. And, of course, the books must be kept, so don't minimize the contribution of accountants specializing in architectural work.

While we're in this area, we must not forget the roles played by architects who have moved into the legal and insurance parts of the building industry.

There are many more. Computer programmers, systems analysts, specification writers, statisticians, administrators, estimators, technicians, and other assorted specialists—all play important parts in the business of building a better world. If you are interested enough to investigate, they can also play important parts in your world and your career selection plans.

8

A LOOK INTO TOMORROW

If we look into the "crystal ball" called the *Occupational Outlook Handbook,* published by the U.S. Department of Labor, we find that prospects for architects are expected to be favorable through the mid-1980's. Employment of architects is expected to rise at a much faster rate than the average for all workers during this period. In recent years, the number of degrees granted in architecture also has been increasing rapidly. If this trend continues, the number of people seeking employment in this field should be roughly in balance with the number of openings from growth, deaths, and retirements. The outlook for these workers may change, however, during short-run periods. Since the demand for architects is highly dependent upon the level of new construction, any significant upsurge or downturn in building could temporarily affect the employment scene for architects.

Although the Labor Department feels that most job openings are expected to be in architectural firms, it anticipates that some will occur in colleges and universities, construction firms, and governments, as agencies become more involved with concepts of environmental design and planning.

The major factor contributing to the increase in the employment of architects appears to be the expected rapid growth of nonresidential construction. Projected increases in the number of architectural students should also result in the hiring of additional architects to teach in colleges and universities.

Further opportunities for employment will also be created through growing public concern about the quality of the physical environment. This concern is expected to increase the demand for urban development and city and community environmental planning projects.

Speaking with members of the AIA about the future for architects and architecture, we got similar, though more subdued, answers. They told us, "Generally speaking, the future looks good. The construction industry now accounts for a healthy percentage of America's gross national product. Not all of that construction is professionally designed, by any means —but a larger and larger segment of it will be, as the public gets more sophisticated in its demands for good design, and as professionals realize that there is a whole spectrum of clients who can use their services.

"Architects—with the help of their professional society, the American Institute of Architects—are making their collective voice heard in legislatures and are playing a larger and more effective role as cities, counties, states, and the federal government begin to plan and build on a super-scale. Meanwhile, they are still providing architectural services for growing numbers of private clients.

"While architecture, like every other business (and most professions), is subject to the ups and downs of the national economy, the long-term trend is definitely up."

Nowhere in either prognostication is there any mention of the sex of the architects. Can we assume the future looks equally bright for all architects, male and female? If the women architects and their colleagues at the AIA have anything to say about it, the future for women in architecture couldn't be brighter.

"Brighter than what?" you ask. Anything has to be better than a ludicrous 3.7%. Let's see what a "typical" woman architect is today, so we can judge how far we all must go to make the future brighter. As part of its two-year study, *Women in Architecture,* the AIA worked up a composite and found that in 1973–74 "the 'typical' woman architect was thirty-nine years old, single, and living in the California, New York, New England, or Northwest AIA regions. She was working full time at an annual salary of $14,700, and this was her sole support. If she was among the 43 percent of the women architects who take on freelance work, it added $2,600 to her yearly income.

"She probably works for a firm with fewer than twenty employees and is classified as a project architect or designer/draftsman. She has been with the firm for six years (five at her present position), and it is probably the fourth firm she has worked for in her fourteen-year career. Chances are she is not among the owners of the firm.

"She is probably a registered architect, but she is less likely to be an AIA member—and even less likely to hold an NCARB certificate.

"Architecture was her first choice as a career—a choice she made when she was eighteen years old. She went on to get a Bachelor's degree in architecture, and perhaps a Master's (twice as likely to have done so as her male counterpart), and she intends to continue her professional studies.

"The odds are very good that she would do it all over again, and that she would encourage young people to choose a career in architecture—even though she has had firsthand experience with the many forms of discrimination."

In an earlier chapter we mentioned the AIA Affirmative Action Plan designed to get more women interested in and actually into architecture. Here's how they hope to do it and here's what you can look for over the next several years as you get closer and closer to your goal in the field. These promises and projections may turn out to be your ticket to the career you've dreamed of and will be working so hard to achieve:

"Increasing the number of women in the architectural profession is the first major area for action under the plan. Over the next four years, the plan calls for a change in the image of the architectural profession, from that of a man's profession to one of a profession of both women and men, along with a substantial increase in the number of women architects.

"Fulfilling these objectives calls for the meeting of some specific goals.

"The first is increased public awareness of the contribution of women architects to the design of the built environment. Since the number of women entering the profession is directly related to the number of women entering and graduating from architectural schools, the plan calls for a rise in the percentage

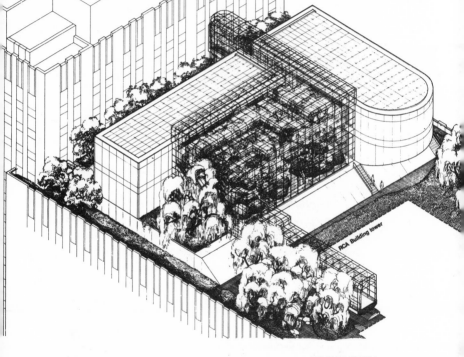

MARLYS HANN

Plans like these, for a complete complex, from a well-known woman architect will become more and more commonplace as women take their deserved place in architecture

enrollment of women in all architectural programs (graduate and undergraduate). In 1976–77, according to the plan, women students should account for 10 percent of total enrollment; that figure should rise over four years to reach 23 percent by 1979–80.

"The rate of graduation of women architecture students should also rise, but there is still not yet enough statistical information to set percentage goals. The proportion of women faculty members is also to be increased, to 10 percent of total faculty the first year and to 15 percent by the third year. And the existing policy in all AIA scholarship programs and Institute Scholar Programs is, of course, to be maintained.

"Throughout all AIA documents, publications, and communications—written or spoken—the profession will be represented as a profession made up of men and women. It will be promoted as open to women as well as to men, and the work of women architects will be publicized.

"A package of material on women architects and their work is to be developed to be made available to all interested groups. Career guidance materials will be collected, cataloged, and distributed on request, and AIA is to work with the National American Personnel and Guidance Association to develop an information program on architectural careers that will clear up misconceptions about requirements for entering the profession. And women architects are to visit and lecture in architectural schools under a pilot program funded by AIA."

That seems to cover all the bases concerning changing the image of architecture from a "male-dominated bastion" to a profession that encourages participation by all qualified aspirants, female or male. But what about the existing inequities in hiring, in salaries, and in a whole host of other employment practices? What about opportunities for women architects competing as architects, and not as *women* architects? What about the attitudes of practicing male *and practicing female* architects on the abilities and opportunities for women in architecture? Are women their own worst enemies? Heeding its own survey, the AIA has endorsed the following actions. You and all other interested persons will have to determine whether this endorsement is just words, or whether equality has truly come to all in architecture.

"In the next four years the plan calls for the narrowing of the gap between women's salaries and men's. Women's salaries should reach 70 percent of men's salaries in 1976, increasing each year until they are 90 percent of men's salaries in 1979. From that point on, there should be complete parity.

"The gap in starting salaries is to be completely closed by 1979. The proportion of women among the ranks of registered architects is also to be increased—to 2.5 percent in 1976 and to 5 percent by 1979. And all AIA members are to be brought up to date on the principles and practices involved in equal employment opportunities.

"Specific actions in the area of equal employment opportunities include offering materials and activities related to equal employment opportunity . . . incorporating guidelines on employment practices into the Handbook of Professional Practice, and developing articles on the legal and ethical aspects of employment discrimination for the AIA Journal.

"AIA's benefit insurance programs are to be reviewed for compliance with employment legislation, and current guidelines and policies on employment discrimination. Noncompliances are to be corrected by 1978.

"Another action will be to involve more women at all levels of the Intern Development Program. The pilot program will be studied for special difficulties that might be encountered by women interns, and all material prepared for the program will reflect AIA policy on women in the profession.

"Through its component assistance programs, AIA is to help promote state registration laws and procedures that will not discriminate against women. Qualified women will be sought for the Summer Legal Intern program."

What else can you look for and hope for in your chosen career in architecture? Happily for you, at this time, it doesn't seem as if the AIA has missed much after accepting the findings of its Task Force on Women in Architecture. The Institute is, however, most unhappy about the very, very small number (out of the rather small number of women architects) who have become members of the AIA. Here's what they say on that subject.

"Disaffection for the Institute on the part of women members, and lack of interest by women who are potential members, is not just a problem for the individual professional herself. It also represents a considerable loss of talent, energy, and experience that the AIA and its components need.

"Over the next four years, the plan calls for the addition of more women to the membership roster, and for their full participation in all activities and at all levels of the Institute.

"Specifically, the plan calls for the number of women members to increase at a rate faster than the overall rate of membership growth, along with an increase (in percentage and in number) in the women chairing or serving on national AIA committees.

"The plan calls for 19.5 percent of the women members to be on committees; by 1979 that percentage is expected to rise to 25 percent. And the proportion of women in all AIA activities and programs is to rise. The plan also provides for help for components in setting up their own affirmative action plans starting in at least nine regions (where the numbers of women architects are greatest) in 1976, and expanding to all regions in 1977.

"To meet these goals, AIA is expected to help regional directors and commission chairpersons find qualified women for committee assignments and participation in all AIA activities. Encouragement will be given to participation in the annual convention by women architects and others at the lower end of the salary range. Convention activities will be used to promote AIA's policy on equal employment and professional opportunities: a Woman Architects' Caucus to review the AAP, and informal meetings of women architects with students and your professionals.

"References presenting architects or AIA members as solely male will be eliminated from AIA publications. The removal of such sexist language has begun in new publications; it will start in membership and application forms by the end of January, and in reissues of previously published material throughout the next four years, AIA's policy of discouraging sex-oriented advertisements in product information will also be continued.

"Other actions in this area include an Affirmative Action Clearinghouse to collect information on the AAP and other programs designed to encourage greater participation by women; funds for a consultant to help the Institute put the plan into action; an information exchange between AIA and organizations of women in architecture, including AIA representatives at significant women architects' events, and the active promotion of the plan throughout the membership and organization of AIA."

That's the AIA plan. How much effect it will have remains to be seen. Unfortunately, as we previously suggested, in many instances and situations women have been their own worst enemy. They have, for the most part, been unwilling to try to break down the barriers of sex discrimination in architecture, as in other professions. They have, as one woman said, "taken plenty of garbage" because fighting would have meant losing jobs. They have been "walked all over," accepted lower status, lower pay, and far fewer opportunities in the hope that somehow, somewhere, someday, they could get "their big break."

These situations are diminishing and, in many cases, ending. Women are now standing up for what's right and fair with far less fear of recrimination, and where there *is* recrimination, they are going back or standing tall or going to the courts and fighting it. In the future we can therefore expect more and more equality in direct relation to the amount of offensive action taken by women against discrimination wherever and whenever it occurs.

One of the best ways to make the future considerably brighter is for women to find out about themselves and each other, to share mutual problems and "compare notes." It is vital that women take advantage of each opportunity to share experiences, frustrations, and successes. One award-winning architect said, "We need to talk about our situation. We must realize that we don't have to be 'perfect' or 'great' to have an impact on our profession. We all certainly know enough male architects who aren't especially outstanding."

Several organizations and associations have been formed in various parts of the country for women architects. It is important that you know about them and join them when you are ready, for your own professional growth and success as well as that of other women. Support them and understand that they are available to help you in many different ways. Check the list in the Appendix for some of these organizations. And if you feel a need in your specialty or your geographic location and there is no group to help, do what other professional women are now doing all over the country—start your own.

One group you should know about and seriously consider joining is the Woman's School of Planning and Architecture. Perhaps even now is not too soon. Completely founded, financed, and run by women, this two-week summer school grew from the experiences and convictions of seven women who met through other professional organizations. Its purpose, according to the coordinators, is "to create a personally supportive atmosphere for the free exchange of ideas and knowledge, and to encourage both professional and personal growth through a fuller integration of our values and identities as women with our values and indentities as designers. The school is committed to discovering and defining the particular qualities, concerns, and abilities which we as women can bring to our work in the environmental design professions. We seek to provide a sharing, nonjudgmental, and noncompetitive atmosphere, and a learning experience where the participants' varied ages and experiences are a major educational resource. We have seen that the diversity among participants can illuminate and expand the common experiences we share as women in a male-dominated society and professions."

The courses offered at one session included many of obvious and immediate use to anyone interested in a rewarding career in architecture: Women and the Built Environment; The Politics

At the Woman's School of Planning and Architecture a brainstorming session from a course called "Women and the Built Environment" results in an architectural program for future students

and Ideology of the Planning Process; A Feminist Analysis of Design Methods and Content; Energy-conscious Design: The Integration of the Natural and Built Environment; Writing for Designers: The Writing Process as a Communication Tool; Exploring Basic Woodworking Techniques; The Design and Construction of Architectural Tapestry; The Use of Videotape for Documentation and Design; and The Role of Women in Local Planning Issues.

Another valuable approach to helping women in architecture to achieve the levels they deserve comes from some forward-thinking schools of architecture that have initiated special courses in their curriculum. If the school you have selected has such courses, take them. If it does not, show "the powers that be" this description of Pratt Institute's course "Women in Architecture," and see if you can start one like it at your school:

"The course is necessary to make women students aware of themselves and their worth in today's field, which, in turn, brings awareness to others, both female and male. The course is divided into thrée concurrently taught approaches: Women

Special courses in down-to-earth subjects at WSPA give present and future architects hands-on training so they can better understand construction problems

as Architects, Women as Users, Women as Architectural Alternatives.

"Under these topics one would deal with problems as ranging as: combining career, marriage, and motherhood; career counseling; and contemporary and historical research into contribution of women architects.

"Relating the course to design, it will deal with special building types, i.e., day care centers, birth and abortion clinics, and also explore the question of 'is there a feminine or feminist way of designing?' "

Most of these are things you can look for and do a bit later in your education or career. What can you do right now to help move you toward a bright future in architecture?

Perhaps the first and most obvious step might be to take advantage of the new AIA career development programs currently visiting high schools. Contact the AIA and make arrangements for them to visit your school. Then make it your business to meet and talk to as many architects as you can find. Most people have never met an architect. We all know about doctors, lawyers, and other professionals, but have never met or had any contact with a living, breathing architect. Don't you be one of these people.

Then—and perhaps most important, if you are truly serious about a career in this profession—consider starting a "Future Professional Women of America" club in your school for the women who have chosen to enter the professions.

With or without the assistance of an adviser, your organization can invite professional women to come into the school, set up programs and generally educate, discuss, and encourage young women to enter the professions. Women doctors, architects, lawyers, dentists, CPA's, engineers, and others will be delighted to spend an afternoon talking to your friends. Remember, women work just as long as men. Stop thinking about "a job" and start preparing for a career.

If you want to succeed, the time for action is now and the place is wherever you are standing at this moment. The future, *your* future, is right around the corner and getting closer and

99

closer. Because of the time, the work, and the struggles of other women and men in architecture, your road will be just a little smoother.

Now it's your turn. Get started. Get moving along the path that you've chosen, the one that leads to the business card that reads, "Ms.—Architect."

APPENDIX
Abbreviations

Degrees

B.A.	Bachelor of Arts
B.Arch.	Bachelor of Architecture. (Normally the first professional degree—"the Bachelor's")
B.Des.	Bachelor of Design
B.E.D.	Bachelor of Environmental Design
B.F.A.	Bachelor of Fine Arts
B.I.A.	Bachelor of Interior Architecture
B.I.D.	Bachelor of Interior (Industrial) Design
B.L.A.	Bachelor of Landscape Architecture
B.S.	Bachelor of Science
B.S.A.E.	Bachelor of Architectural Engineering
B.S.C.E.	Bachelor of Construction Engineering
B.U.P.	Bachelor of Urban Planning
M.A.	Master of Arts
M.A.A.	Master of Arts (Architecture)
M.Arch.	Master of Architecture. (May be the first professional degree in six-year program—"the Master's")

M.B.C.	Master of Building Construction
M.B.S.	Master of Building Science
M.C.P.	Master of City Planning
M.F.A.	Master of Fine Arts
M.P.S.U.P.	Master of Architecture and Urban Planning
M.R.P.	Master of Regional Planning (and combinations)
M.S.	Master of Science
M.U.D.	Master of Urban Design (and combinations)
M.U.P.	Master of Urban Planning
Ph.D.	Doctor of Philosophy

Other Abbreviations

ACSA	Association of Collegiate Schools of Architecture
ACT	American College Test
AIA	American Institute of Architects
ASLA	American Society of Landscape Architects
CEEB	College Entrance Examination Board
FAS	Federation of American Scientists
GPA	Grade Point Average
GRE	Graduate Record Examination
NAAB	National Architectural Accrediting Board
NCARB	National Council of Architectural Registration Boards
SAT	Scholastic Aptitude Test

American Colleges and Universities Offering Programs in Architecture and Related Subjects

The list that follows contains the names, addresses, and pertinent admission and financial information for schools in the United States conducting programs in architecture and related subjects at the time of publication. The information was gathered from the schools and from a variety of other sources. All entries, including tuition and room and board, are minimum estimates. More detailed information should be obtained from the individual schools.

Arizona State University, College of Architecture
    Tempe, Arizona 85281
        Degrees granted
            B.Arch., 5 years; M.Arch., 1 year
        Expenses
            Yearly tuition, $370 resident; $1,370 out of state; room and board, $1,100; other expenses, $900
        Women students
            5%

University of Arizona, College of Architecture
    Tucson, Arizona 85721
        Degrees granted
            B.Arch., 5 years; M.Arch., 6 years
        Requirements
            ACT
        Expenses
            Yearly tuition, $450 resident; $1,640 out of state; room and board, $1,175; other expenses, $400
        Women students
            8%

Auburn University, School of Architecture and Fine Arts
Department of Architecture
    Auburn, Alabama 96880
        Degrees granted
            B.S. in Env. Des. (nonprofessional), 4 years; B.Arch., 5 years
        Requirements
            ACT or SAT; college prep math
        Expenses
            Yearly tuition, $549 resident; $1,074 out of state; room and board, $1,350; other expenses, $300
        Women students
            7%

Ball State University, College of Architecture and Planning
Muncie, Indiana 47306
Degrees granted
B.Arch., 5 years; B.L.A., 5 years
Requirements
Upper quarter of high school class; SAT
Expenses
Yearly tuition, $720 resident; $1,440 out of state; room and board, $1,124; other expenses, $625
Women students
Undergraduate, 5%

Boston Architectural Center, 320 Newbury Street
Boston, Massachusetts 02115
Degrees granted
Certificate; 6 years (evenings)
Expenses
Yearly tuition, $580 first year; all others, $530
Women students
32%

University of California—Berkeley, College of Environmental Design
Berkeley, California 94720
Degrees granted
B.A., 4 years; M.Arch., 6 years; M.Arch., 1 to 3 years; M.C.P., 2 years; M.L.A., 2 years; B.I.D., 4 years; M.I.D., 1 to 2 years
Requirements
At least B average in required courses of last three years of high school
Expenses
Yearly tuition, $637.50 resident undergraduate; $2,137.50 out of state; $697.50 resident graduate; $2,197.50 out of state; room and board, $1,827; other expenses, $800
Women students
12%

University of California—Los Angeles, School of Architecture and Urban Planning
Los Angeles, California 90024
Degrees granted
M.Arch., 2 to 3 years
Requirements
3.0 GPA last two years of college
Expenses
Yearly tuition, $681 resident; $2,181 out of state; room and board, $1,300; other expenses, $700
Women students
21%

California Polytechnic State University, School of Architecture and Environmental Design
San Luis Obispo, California 93401
Degrees granted
B.Arch., 5 years; M.Arch., 6 years; B.S. in Arch. Eng., 4 years; B.S.

in Arch., 4 years; B.S. in C.R.P., 4 years; B.S. in C.Eng., 4 years; B.S. in L.A., 4 years; M.S. in Arch., 1 year; M.S. in C.R.P., 1 year

Requirements

California residents *only.* Upper third of high school class; SAT or ACT

Expenses

Yearly tuition, $576; room and board, $1,539; other expenses, $600

Women students

10%

California State Polytechnic University, School of Environmental Design
Pomona, California 91768

Degrees granted

B.S. in Arch., 4 years; M.Arch., 6 years; B.U.P., 4 years; M.U.P., 2 years; B.S. in L.A., 4 years; M.L.A., 2 years

Requirements

State residents only. Upper third of high school class

Expenses

Yearly tuition, $210 resident; room and board, $1,356; other expenses, $450

Women students

4%

Carnegie-Mellon University, Department of Architecture
Pittsburgh, Pennsylvania 15213

Degrees granted

B.Arch., 4 to 5 years; M.Arch., degree plus 3 years; B.F.A.(Arch.), 4 years

Requirements

SAT or ACT; Architectural School Aptitude Test

Expenses

Yearly tuition, $2,900; room and board, $1,575; other expenses, $675

Catholic University of America, School of Engineering and Architecture
Department of Architecture and Planning
Washington, D.C. 20017

Degrees granted

M.Arch., 5 years; 1 year full-time residence

Requirements

Evidence of qualification, portfolio, and description of professional experience

Expenses

Yearly tuition, $3,800 (comprehensive fee); other expenses, $400

Women students

Graduate, 20%; undergraduate, 12%

University of Cincinnati, College of Design, Architecture, and Art
Department of Architecture
Cincinnati, Ohio 45221

Degrees granted

B.Arch., 6 years; B.U.P., 5 years

Requirements

Upper half of high school class; SAT or ACT

Expenses
>Yearly tuition, $795 Cincinnati resident; $930 non-Cincinnati, but Ohio resident; $1,905 out of state; room and board, $1,542; other expenses, $400

Women students
>5%

City College of the City University of New York, School of Architecture and Environmental Studies
* New York, New York 10031
>*Degrees granted*
>>B.S. in Arch., 4 years; B.Arch., 5 years; M.U.P., 1 year

>*Expenses*
>>Yearly tuition, $116 resident; $1,200 out of state

>*Women students*
>>10%

Clemson University, College of Architecture
>Clemson, South Carolina 29631
>>*Degrees granted*
>>>B.S. (pre-Arch.), 4 years; B.A. (pre-Arch.), 4 years; B.Arch., 5 years; M.Arch., 2 years; M.C.R.P., 2 years plus summer

>>*Requirements*
>>>High school diploma; interviews

>>*Expenses:*
>>>Yearly tuition, $640 resident; $1,340 out of state; room and board, $880; other expenses, $200

>>*Women students*
>>>7%

University of Colorado, College of Environmental Design
>Boulder, Colorado 80302
>>*Degrees granted*
>>>B.E.D., 4 years; B.Arch., 5 years; M.Arch., 1 or 2 years

>>*Expenses*
>>>Yearly tuition, $638 resident; $2,070 out of state; room and board, $1,295

>>*Women students*
>>>9%

Columbia University, Graduate School of Architecture and Planning
>New York, New York 10027
>>*Degrees granted*
>>>M.Arch., 3 years; M.S. in Arch. and U.D., 2 years; M.S. in Arch. Tech., 1 year; M.S. in U.P., 2 years; Ph.D. in U.P. (varies)

>>*Requirements*
>>>Degrees or at least 60 credits in liberal arts; aptitude test or GRE

>>*Expenses*
>>>Yearly tuition, $4,215; room and board, $2,300; other expenses, $700

>>*Women students*
>>>33%

Cooper Union, 41 Cooper Square
New York, New York 10003

Degrees granted
    B.Arch., 5 years
Requirements
    SAT; home project
Expenses
    No tuition, $200 annual student fee; other expenses, $500
Women students
    17%

Cornell University, College of Architecture, Art, and Planning
  Ithaca, New York 14853
    Degrees granted
        B.Arch., 5 years; B.F.A., 4 years; M.Arch., B.Arch. plus 2 years; M.S.,
        Bachelor's plus 1 year; M.A., Ph.D., M.L.A., or M.C.R.P. (varies)
    Requirements
        SAT or ACT; 3 years of foreign language
    Expenses
        Yearly tuition, $4,110; room and board, $2,000; other expenses,
        $700
    Women students
        16%

University of Detroit, School of Architecture, 4001 W. McNichols Road
  Detroit, Michigan 48221
    Degrees granted
        B.S. in Arch., 4 years; M.Arch., degree plus 2 years
    Requirements
        SAT or ACT; B average in high school
    Expenses
        Yearly tuition, $2,550; room and board, $1,700; other expenses,
        $100
    Women students
        8%

Drexel University, 32d and Chestnut Streets
  Philadelphia, Pennsylvania 19104
    Degrees granted
        B.S., 7 years
    Requirements
        High school diploma
    Expenses
        Yearly tuition, $2,265; room and board, $1,215; other expenses,
        $600
    Women students
        3%

University of Florida, College of Architecture and Fine Arts
  Gainesville, Florida 32611
    Degrees granted
        B.Des., 4 years; M.A.Arch., 6 years; B.L.A., 4 years; B.B.C., 4 years
    Requirements
        Resident: high school diploma, C average, top 40% on Florida
        Twelfth Grade Tests. Out of state: same as above, plus priority given
        to scorers of over 1,000 on SAT and high school average of B or
        better

107

Expenses
Yearly tuition, $843 resident; $1,893 out of state; room and board, $1,300; other expenses, $650
Women students
6%

Georgia Institute of Technology, College of Architecture
Atlanta, Georgia 30332
Degrees granted
B.S., 4 years; B.I.D., 4 years; B.Arch., 5 years; B.S. in B.C., 4 years; M.S., 2 years; M. Arch., 6 years; M.C.P., 2 years
Requirements
High school diploma and SAT
Expenses
Yearly tuition, $676.50 resident; $1,843.50 out of state; room and board, $1,300; other expenses, $200
Women students
14%

Hampton Institute, Department of Architecture
Hampton, Virginia 23368
Degrees granted
B.Arch., 5 years
Requirements
Upper half of high school graduating class; SAT
Expenses
Yearly tuition, $1,770; room and board, $860; other expenses, $500
Women students
4%

Harvard University, Dept. of Architecture, Graduate School of Design
Cambridge, Massachusetts 02138
Degrees granted
M.Arch., 3.5 years; M.L.A., 2 years; M.C.P., 2 years; M.R.P., 2 years; M.Arch. in U.D., 2 years; M.L.A. (U.D.), 2 years; M.C.P. (U.D.), 2 years
Requirements
B.A., B.S., or Bachelor's degree in specific area
Expenses
Yearly tuition, $3,450; room and board, $1,480; other expenses, $500
Women students
35%

University of Hawaii, Department of Architecture
Honolulu, Hawaii 96822
Degrees granted
M.Arch., 2 years; M.Arch. in U.D., 1½ years; M.Arch. in Arch. Eng., 2 years
Expenses
Yearly tuition, $336 resident; $819 out of state; room and board, $852; other expenses, $1,000
Women students
8%

108

University of Houston, College of Architecture
  Houston, Texas 77004
    Degrees granted
      B.Arch., 5 years
    Expenses
      Yearly tuition, $300 resident; $1,160 out of state; room and board,
      $1,282
    Women students
      8%

Howard University, School of Engineering and Architecture
  Washington, D.C. 20001
    Degrees granted
      B.Arch., 5 years; M.C.P., 1 year
    Expenses
      Yearly tuition, $1,360; room and board, $1,330; other expenses,
      $250
    Women students
      8%

University of Idaho, Department of Arts and Architecture
  Moscow, Idaho 83843
    Degrees granted
      B.L.A., 4 years; B.Arch., 5 years; M.Arch.
    Requirements
      M.Arch: B.Arch. plus portfolio and résumé
    Expenses
      Yearly tuition, $380 resident; $1,380 out of state; room and board,
      $1,060; other expenses, $600 plus
    Women students
      8%

Idaho State University, Department of Architecture
  Pocatello, Idaho 83201
    Degrees granted
      B.Arch., 5 years
    Expenses
      Yearly tuition, $400 resident; $1,250 out of state; room and board,
      $1,005; other expenses, $100
    Women students
      2%

University of Illinois, Chicago Circle Campus, Department of Architecture
  Chicago, Illinois 60680
    Degrees granted
      M.Arch., 5 years; M.Arch., degree plus 2 years
    Requirements
      Degree plus GPA of 3.75 (A=5.0)
    Expenses
      Yearly tuition, $666 resident; $1,656 out of state; other expenses,
      $700
    Women students
      9%

University of Illinois, Urbana-Champaign, Department of Architecture
Urbana, Illinois 61801
Degrees granted
B.Arch., 5 years; M.Arch., degree plus 2 years or B. Arch. plus 1 year
Requirements
Graduate GPA 4.0 (on 5.0 scale)
Expenses
Yearly tuition, $686 resident; $1,676 out of state; room and board, $1,182 women; $1,222 men; other expenses, $750
Women students
12%

Illinois Institute of Technology, School of Architecture and Planning
Chicago, Illinois 60616
Degrees granted
B.Arch., 5 years; M.Arch., 2 years; B.C.R.P., 4 years; M.C.R.P., 2 to 3 years
Requirements
Upper half of high school class
Expenses
Freshmen and sophomores, $2,300; others, $2,500; room and board, $1,250; other expenses, $600
Women students
11%

Iowa State University, College of Engineering, Dept. of Architecture
Ames, Iowa 50011
Degrees granted
B.Arch., 4 years; M.Arch., 6 years
Requirements
B.A. in Arch.: students must be in upper half of their class. Also: a curriculum vitae, official transcripts, short personal statement, short explanation of proposed thesis topic, three letters of recommendation, examples of applicant's work.
Expenses
Yearly tuition, $774 resident; $1,650 out of state; room and board, $990; other expenses, $700
Women students
6%

University of Kansas, School of Architecture and Urban Design
Lawrence, Kansas 66044
Degrees granted
B.S. in Env. Des., 4 years; B.Arch., 5 years; B.S. in Arch. Eng., 4 years; M.Arch., 2 years; M.S. in Arch. Eng., 1 year
Expenses
Yearly tuition, $573 resident; $1,363 out of state; room and board, $1,250; other expenses, $600
Women students
6%

Kansas State University, College of Architecture and Design
Manhattan, Kansas 66506

110

Degrees granted
B.Arch., 5 years; B.I.A., 5 years; B.L.A., 5 years; M.R.C.P., M.Arch., M.L.A.
Requirements
Resident: Kansas high school diploma; ACT. Out of state: ACT comprehensive score of 25; high class rank
Expenses
Yearly tuition, $532 resident; $1,322 out of state; room and board, $1,120; other expenses, $500
Women students
13%

Kent State University, School of Architecture and Environmental Design
Kent, Ohio 44242
Degrees granted
B.Arch., 5 years; M.Arch., 6 years
Requirements
Ohio residents: ACT; high school diploma. Out of state: upper half of high school class
Expenses
Yearly tuition, $855 resident; $2,055 out of state; room and board, $1,410; other expenses, $450
Women students
5%

University of Kentucky, College of Architecture
Lexington, Kentucky 40506
Degrees granted
B.Arch., 5 years
Requirements
ACT; Architectural School Aptitude Test
Expenses
Yearly tuition, $240 resident; $605 out of state
Women students
5%

Lawrence Institute of Technology, School of Architecture
Southfield, Michigan 48075
Degrees granted
B.S. in Arch., 4 years; B.Arch., 5 years
Expenses
Yearly tuition, $760

Louisiana State University, School of Environmental Design
Baton Rouge, Louisiana 70803
Degrees granted
B.Arch., 5 years
Expenses
Yearly tuition, $320 resident; $1,050 out of state; room and board, $908
Women students
4%

University of Southwestern Louisiana, School of Art and Architecture
Lafayette, Louisiana 70501

111

Degrees granted
    B.Arch., 5 years
Expenses
    Yearly tuition, $315 resident; $945 out of state; room and board,
    $800; other expenses, $500
Women students
    2%

University of Maryland, School of Architecture
  College Park, Maryland 20742
    Degrees granted
        B.Arch., 5 years
    Requirements
        SAT
    Expenses
        Yearly tuition, $698 resident; $1,848 out of state; room and board,
        $1,120; other expenses, $550
    Women students
        17%

Massachusetts Institute of Technology, School of Architecture and Planning
  Cambridge, Massachusetts 02139
    Degrees granted
        M.C.P., 6 years; M.Arch., 6 years; Ph.D. in Arch. (varies)
    Requirements
        SAT, achievement tests in: math level I or II; physics or chemistry;
        English composition or history
    Expenses
        Yearly tuition, $3,700; room and board, $2,200; other expenses,
        $500
    Women students
        25%

University of Miami, Department of Architecture and Architectural Engineering
  Coral Gables, Florida 33124
    Degrees granted
        B.Arch., 5 years; B.S. in Arch. Eng., 4 years
    Requirements
        SAT
    Expenses
        Yearly tuition, $2,633; room and board, $1,430; other expenses,
        $300
    Women students
        13%

Miami University, School of Fine Arts
  Oxford, Ohio 45056
    Degrees granted
        B.E.D., 4 years; B.Arch., 5 years; M.Arch., 2 years
    Requirements
        High school diploma; SAT; Architectural School Aptitude Test
    Expenses
        Yearly tuition, $840 resident; $2,040 out of state; room and board,
        $1,395; other expenses, $600

112

Women students
10%

University of Michigan, College of Architecture and Urban Planning
Ann Arbor, Michigan 48109
Degrees granted
B.S. in Arch., 4 years; M.Arch., 6 years; D.Arch., 3 years; M.U.P.,
2 years
Requirements
High school diploma; completion of pre-professional requirements;
interview; portfolio
Expenses
Yearly tuition, $1,052 resident; $3,252 out of state; room and board,
$1,650; other expenses, $1,202
Women students
15%

University of Minnesota, School of Architecture and Landscape Architecture
Minneapolis, Minnesota 55455
Degrees granted
B.Arch., 5 years; M.Arch., 6 years; B.E.D., 4 years (nonprofessional);
B.A. in Arch., 4 years (nonprofessional)
Requirements
Application and admission for one year in either Institute of Technol-
ogy or College of Liberal Arts
Expenses
Yearly tuition, $3,000 resident; $4,300 out of state; room and board,
$1,540; other expenses $200
Women students
9%

Montana State University, College of Arts and Architecture
Bozeman, Montana 59715
Degrees granted
B.Arch., 5 years
Requirements
High school diploma; out of state: upper 50% of high school class
Expenses
Yearly tuition, $510 resident; $972 out of state; room and board,
$1,179; other expenses, $250
Women students
2%

University of Nebraska—Lincoln, College of Architecture
Lincoln, Nebraska 68508
Degrees granted
B.S. in Arch. Studies, 4 years; M.Arch., 2 years
Requirements
Residents: high school diploma; ACT or SAT scores. Out of state: high
school diploma; ACT or SAT scores; top half of high school class
Expenses
Yearly tuition, $663 resident; $1,563 out of state; room and board,
$1,095; other expenses, $842
Women students
2%

113

New Jersey School of Architecture, New Jersey Institute of Technology
323 High Street, Newark, New Jersey 07102
Degrees granted
B.Arch., 2 years college plus 3 years
Expenses
Yearly tuition, $960; other expenses, $200
Women students
33%

University of New Mexico, College of Fine Arts
Albuquerque, New Mexico 87106
Degrees granted
B.F.A. (Arch.), 4 years; M.Arch., 2 to 3 years
Expenses
Yearly tuition, $456 resident; $1,284 out of state; room and board,
$1,240; other expenses, $800
Women students
10%

N.Y. Institute of Technology, Division of Architecture and Arts, Department of
Architecture
Old Westbury, New York 11568
Degrees granted
B.Arch., 5 years; B.S. in Arch. Tech., 4 years
Requirements
SAT
Expenses
Yearly tuition, $2,200; other expenses, $250
Women students
4%

State University of New York at Buffalo, School of Architecture and Environ-
mental Design
Buffalo, New York 14214
Degrees granted
M.Arch., 2 to 3 years; B.E.D., 2 to 3 years; B. of professional studies
in Arch., 2 to 3 years
Requirements
Two years of college, including 24 hours pre-architecture
Expenses
Yearly tuition, undergraduate, $900 resident; $1,500 out of state;
graduate, $1,400 resident; $1,800 out of state; room and board,
$913
Women students
Undergraduate, 22%; graduate, 23%

University of North Carolina—Charlotte, College of Architecture
Charlotte, North Carolina 28223
Degrees granted
B.A. in Arch., 4 years; B.Arch., degree plus 1 year
Expenses
Yearly tuition, $413 resident; $1,973 out of state; room and board,
$965; other expenses, $400

114

North Carolina State University, School of Design
Raleigh, North Carolina 27607
Degrees granted
B.E.D. in Arch., 4 years; M.Arch., 2 years; M.U.D., 2 years; M.L.A.,
2 years
Expenses
Yearly tuition, $487 resident; $2,033 out of state; room and board,
$775; other expenses, $550
Women students
9%

North Dakota State University, Department of Architecture
Fargo, North Dakota 58102
Degrees granted
B.A. or B.S. in Arch. Studies, 4 years; B.A. in Arch., 5 years; M.Arch.,
2 years
Requirements
ACT
Expenses
Yearly tuition, $435 resident; $1,164 out of state; room and board,
$1,000; other expenses, $400
Women students
4%

University of Notre Dame, Department of Architecture
Notre Dame, Indiana 46556
Degrees granted
B.Arch., 5 years; M.S. in E.D., 2 years
Expenses
° Yearly tuition, $2,782; room and board, $1,224 for men; $1,088 for
women; other expenses, $500
Women students
4%

Ohio State University, School of Architecture
Columbus, Ohio 43210
Degrees granted
B.S. in Arch., 4 years; M.Arch., 2 years; M.C.P., 2 years; B.S. in L.A.,
4 years
Requirements
SAT
Expenses
Yearly tuition, $780 resident undergraduate; $1,830 out of state;
$930 resident graduate; $2,010 out of state; room and board,
$1,474; other expenses, $300
Women students
6%

Ohio University, School of Architecture, Design, and Planning
Athens, Ohio 45701
Degrees granted
B.A. in Arch., 4 years; B.Arch., 5 years; M.Arch., 2 years; M.R.P., 2
years

115

Expenses
    Yearly tuition, $780 resident; $1,900 out of state; room and board, $1,419; other expenses, $460
Women students
    11%

University of Oklahoma, College of Environmental Design
    Norman, Oklahoma 73019
    Degrees granted
        B.Arch., 5 years; M.Arch., 6 years (degree plus two years); M.R.C.P., 6 years
    Expenses
        Yearly tuition, $448 resident; $1,280 out of state; room and board, $1,000
    Women students
        1%

Oklahoma State University, School of Architecture
    Stillwater, Oklahoma 74074
    Degrees granted
        B.S. in Arch. Studies, 4 years; M.Arch., degree plus 2 years; M.Arch. Eng., degree plus 2 years
    Requirements
        Residents: high school diploma; ACT scores; high school average of 3.0 or top half of class. Out of state: same, except must have been in top half of class
    Expenses
        Yearly tuition, $456 resident; $1,408 out of state; room and board, $1,100
    Women students
        6%

University of Oregon, School of Architecture and Applied Arts, Dept. of Architecture
    Eugene, Oregon 97403
    Degrees granted
        B.I.A., 5 years; B.Arch., 5 years; M.Arch. (see requirements)
    Requirements
        M.Arch.: Option 1—Requires B.Arch.; takes 4 to 6 terms; Option 2 —Requires A.B. or B.S. *not* in Architecture; takes 9 terms; Option 3 —Does not require degree; requires well-documented arch. experience
    Expenses
        Yearly tuition, undergraduate resident of Oregon, $645; undergraduate nonresident, $1,899; graduate student, $957; room and board, $1,120
    Women students
        Undergraduate, 22%; graduate, 32%

University of Pennsylvania, Graduate School of Fine Arts, Dept. of Architecture
    Philadelphia, Pennsylvania 19104
    Degrees granted
        M.Arch., 1 to 3½ years; Ph.D. in Arch. (varies); M.C.P., 2 years; M.R.P., 2 years

116

Requirements
   Bachelor's degree; courses in math, economics, statistics
Expenses
   Yearly tuition, $3,350; room and board, $1,700, other expenses, $700
Women students
   28%

Penn State University, Division of Environmental Design and Planning, Dept. of Architecture
   University Park, Pennsylvania 16802
   Degrees granted
      B.S., 4 years; M.Arch., 5 years
   Requirements
      M.Arch.: B.A. or B.S. with major in architecture, environmental design; B.Arch., 2.5 junior-senior average, 39 credits in design, plus portfolio
   Expenses
      Yearly tuition, $960 resident; $2,160 nonresident; room and board, $1,239; other expenses, $300
   Women students
      25%

Pratt Institute, School of Architecture
   Brooklyn, New York 11205
   Degrees granted
      B.Arch., 5 years; M.Arch., 1 year; M.S. in U.D., 1½ years; M.S. in C.P., 2 years
   Requirements
      SAT or ACT; CEEB achievement tests in English composition and math, levels 1 or 2, portfolio
   Expenses
      Yearly tuition, $3,348; room and board, $2,700; other expenses, $350
   Women students
      Undergraduate, 11%; graduate, 37%

Princeton University, School of Architecture and Urban Planning
   Princeton, New Jersey 08540
   Degrees granted
      B.A. in Arch. & U.P., 4 years; M.Arch.: 3 years plus B.A. or B.S.; or 2 years plus B.A. or B.A. in Arch.; M.U.P., 2 years; M.P.A.U.P., 3 years; Ph.D. in Arch., 4 years; Ph.D. in U.P., 4 years
   Requirements
      Vary according to program
   Expenses
      Yearly tuition, $4,300; room and board, $1,975; other expenses, $750
   Women students
      13%

Rensselaer Polytechnic Institute, School of Architecture
   Troy, New York 12181
   Degrees granted
      B.Arch., 5 years; M.Arch., B.Arch. plus 1 year

117

Expenses
>> Yearly tuition, $3,260; room and board, $1,400; other expenses, $650

Women students
>> 10%

Rhode Island School of Design, Division of Architectural Studies
> Providence, Rhode Island 02903
>> *Degrees granted*
>>> B.Arch., 5 years; B.L.A., 5 years
>>
>> *Expenses*
>>> Yearly tuition, $3,080; room and board, $1,400; other expenses, $240
>>
>> *Women students*
>>> 13%

Rice University, School of Architecture
> Houston, Texas 77001
>> *Degrees granted*
>>> B.Arch., degree plus 2 years; M.Arch., degree plus 1.5 to 3 years; M.Arch. in U.D., degree plus 1.5 to 3 years; D.Arch. (varies)
>>
>> *Requirements*
>>> High school diploma; SAT or ACT; personal interviews
>>
>> *Expenses*
>>> Yearly tuition, $2,300; room and board, $1,850; other expenses, $700
>>
>> *Women students*
>>> 22%

Southern University and A & M College, College of Engineering
Division of Architecture
> Baton Rouge, Louisiana 70813
>> *Degrees granted*
>>> B.Arch., 5 years

University of Southern California, School of Architecture and Arts, Department of Architecture
> Los Angeles, California 90007
>> *Degrees granted*
>>> B.S. in Arch., 4 years; M.Arch., 6 years; M.B.S., 2 years; M.U.D., 2 years
>>
>> *Requirements*
>>> High school record with emphasis on most recent work; quality of SAT or ACT exams; pattern of secondary school courses
>>
>> *Expenses*
>>> Yearly tuition, $1,620; room and board, $1,300
>>
>> *Women students*
>>> 15%

Syracuse University, School of Architecture
> Syracuse, New York 13210
>> *Degrees granted*
>>> B.Arch., 5 years; M.Arch., 1 year
>>
>> *Requirements*
>>> Portfolio; interview

Expenses
Yearly tuition, $3,113; room and board, $1,700; other expenses, $200
Women students
10%

University of Tennessee, School of Architecture
Knoxville, Tennessee 37916
Degrees granted
B.Arch., 5 years
Requirements
Completion of pre-architecture, and maintenance of 2.3 average
Expenses
Yearly tuition, $417 resident; $1,267 out of state; room and board, $1,400; other expenses, $400
Women students
5%

Tennessee State University, Department of Architectural Engineering
Nashville, Tennessee 37203
Degrees granted
B.S. in Arch. Eng., 4 years
Requirements
Residents: ACT of 17; high school average 2.25 (4.0 system). Out of state: ACT of 18; high school average 2.25 (4.0 system)
Expenses
Yearly tuition, $374 resident; $1,214 out of state; room and board, $778
Women students
4%

University of Texas (Arlington), Department of Architecture
Arlington, Texas 76019
Degrees granted
B.S. in Arch., 4 years; M.Arch., 6 years; M.Arch., degree plus 3 years
Requirements
SAT—1,000; top quarter of high school class
Expenses
Yearly tuition, $370 resident; $1,440 out of state; room and board, $1,585; other expenses, $200
Women students
8%

University of Texas at Austin, Dept. of Architecture, University Station
Austin, Texas 78712
Degrees granted
B.Arch., 5-year program, 6-year program; M.Arch., degree plus 3 years
Requirements
SAT over 1,000 score
Expenses
Yearly tuition, $382 resident; $1,462 out of state; room and board, $1,300; other expenses, $718
Women students
8%

119

Texas A & M University, College of Architecture and Environmental Design
College Station, Texas 77843
    Degrees granted
        M.Arch., 2 years; M.U.P., 2 years; B.S. in L.A., 4 years; M.L.A., 1
        year; B.E.D., 4 years
    Requirements
        SAT scores, top half of high school class + 800
    Expenses
        Yearly tuition, $374 resident; $1,670 out of state; room and board,
        $595
    Women students
        6%

Texas Tech. University, College of Engineering, Dept. of Architecture
Lubbock, Texas 79409
    Degrees granted
        B.Arch., 5 years
    Requirements
        SAT or ACT for residents; out of state applicants need one of these
        exams and must be ranked in top half of high school graduating
        class
    Expenses
        Yearly tuition, $522 resident; $1,602 out of state; room and board,
        $1,220; other expenses, $300
    Women students
        6%

Tulane University, School of Architecture
New Orleans, Louisiana 70118
    Degrees granted
        B.Arch., 5 years; M.Arch., 1 year
    Requirements
        High school diploma; CEEB tests
    Expenses
        Yearly tuition, $3,040; room and board, $1,300; other expenses,
        $500
    Women students
        20%

Tuskegee Institute, School of Applied Sciences
Tuskegee Institute, Alabama 36088
    Degrees granted
        B.A. in Arch. Science, 4 years; M.Arch., 6 years
    Requirements
        SAT or ACT
    Expenses
        Yearly tuition, $1,200; room and board, $800; other expenses, $200
    Women students
        7%

University of Utah, Graduate School of Architecture
Salt Lake City, Utah 84112
    Degrees granted
        M.Arch., 6 years

120

Requirements
   B.A. or B.S. here or elsewhere
Expenses
   Yearly tuition, $525 resident; $1,380 out of state; room and board,
   $1,321; other expenses, $300
Women students
   20%

University of Virginia, School of Architecture
   Charlottesville, Virginia 22903
   Degrees granted
      B.S. in Arch., 4 years; M.Arch., 6 years; B.C.P., 4 years; M.L.A., 2
      years; B.S. in Arch. Hist., 4 years; M. Arch. Hist., 1 year
   Requirements
      SAT
   Expenses
      Yearly tuition, $649 resident; $1,569 out of state; room and board,
      $1,200; other expenses, $600
   Women students
      17%

Virginia Polytechnic Institute and State University, College of Architecture
   Blacksburg, Virginia 24061
   Degrees granted
      B.Arch., 5 years; M.Arch., 6 years; M.U.P.P., 2 years; M.Arch. in
      U.D., 2 years; B.L.A., 5 years
   Requirements
      SAT; CEEB achievement test in English and math
   Expenses
      Yearly tuition, $627 resident; $1,227 out of state; room and board,
      $978; other expenses, $300
   Women students
      8%

University of Washington, College of Architecture and Urban Planning
   Seattle, Washington 98195
   Degrees granted
      B.A. in E.D., 4 years; B.Arch., 5 years; M.Arch., 6 years
   Requirements
      Washington Pre-College Test, plus ACT or SAT; 2.50 GPA, resident;
      3.00 GPA, out of state
   Expenses
      Yearly tuition, $564 resident; $1,581 out of state; room and board,
      $1,200; other expenses, $700
   Women students
      11%

Washington State University, Dept. of Architecture
   Pullman, Washington 99163
   Degrees granted
      B.Arch., 5 years
   Requirements
      SAT; resident, GPA 2.4 (4.0 system); out of state, 3.0

121

Expenses
Yearly tuition, $564 resident; $1,581 out of state; room and board, $1,200; other expenses, $550
Women students
3%

Washington University, School of Architecture
St. Louis, Missouri 63130
Degrees granted
M.Arch., 6 years; M.Arch. and U.D., Bachelor's plus 1.5 years; M.Arch. or M.B.A., Bachelor's plus 3 years; M.Arch. or Master of Social Work, Bachelor's plus 3 years
Requirements
SAT or ACT
Expenses
Yearly tuition, $3,350; room and board, $1,708
Women students
30%

University of Wisconsin—Milwaukee, School of Architecture and Urban Planning
Milwaukee, Wisconsin 53201
Degrees granted
B.S. in Arch. Studies, 4 years; M.Arch., degree plus 2 or 3 years
Requirements
Pre-architecture plus 2.75 GPA
Expenses
Yearly tuition,$573 freshman and sophomore residents; $648 junior and senior residents; $1,906 freshmen and sophomore out of state; $2,204 junior and senior out of state; room and board, $1,502; other expenses, $1,200
Women students
5%

Yale University, School of Architecture
New Haven, Connecticut 06520
Degrees granted
M.Arch., 3 years plus degree
Requirements
B.A., B.S., or in special cases completion of 3 years of a 5-year program, or completion of 4 years of a 5-year program. GRE scores plus portfolio
Expenses
Yearly tuition, $3,950; room and board: dormitory—$800–900; board—cafeteria operated on cash basis
Women students
Graduate, 19%

Women's Architectural Organizations

AIA Task Force on Women in Architecture
  Ms. Judith Edelman
  434 Sixth Avenue
  New York, NY 10011

Alliance of Women in Architecture (AWA)
  41 East 65th Street
  New York, NY 10021

Archive of Women in Architecture
  The Architectural League
  41 East 65th Street
  New York, NY 10021

Bay Area Women Planners
  434 66th Street
  Oakland, CA 94609

Ms. Enid Howarth
  University of New Mexico
  Department of Architecture
  Albuquerque, NM 87106

OWA
  Ms. Pat Noda
  350 Sharon Park Dr., #C6
  Menlo Park, CA 94025

University of Michigan Women in Architecture
  Department of Architecture
  University of Michigan
  Tappen & Monroe
  Ann Arbor, MI 48104

Women Architects, Landscape Architects and Planners (WALAP)
  Boston Architectural Center
  320 Newbury Street
  Boston, MA 02115

Women in Architecture
  College of Architecture
  University of Arizona
  Tucson, AZ 85721
  Attn: Melinda Movius Medlin

Women in Environmental Design
  Ms. Jean Hoops
  219 SW Ash
  Portland, OR 97204

Women of Wurster
  Wurster Hall
  University of California
  Berkeley, CA 94720
  Attn: Ms. Susie Coliver, Architecture

INDEX

126

127

128